The Library PR Handbook
High-Impact Communications

Edited by
Mark R. Gould

AMERICAN LIBRARY ASSOCIATION
CHICAGO   2009

Mark R. Gould, a veteran of twenty-five years in the communication field, has been the director of the American Library Association's Public Information Office since 2000. During his career at ALA, he has focused on the areas of public awareness and partnership development, communication services, media relations, and crisis communication. Gould has received more than a dozen awards from public relations organizations including the International Association of Business Communicators Gold Quill. He was honored in 2007 by the Publicity Club of Chicago for a community relations initiative entitled "Intrepid Librarians Help New Orleans Recover." He has written for the *Chicago Sun-Times, San Francisco Chronicle,* and many other publications.

The paper used in this publication meets the minimum requirements of American National Standard for Information Sciences—Permanence of Paper for Printed Library Materials, ANSI Z39.48-1992. ♾

Library of Congress Cataloging-in-Publication Data
The library PR handbook : high-impact communications / edited by Mark R. Gould.
   p. cm.
  Includes bibliographical references and index.
  ISBN 978-0-8389-1002-3 (alk. paper)
  1. Libraries—Public relations—Handbooks, manuals, etc. 2. Libraries and community—Handbooks, manuals, etc. I. Gould, Mark R.
Z716.3.L52 2009
021.7—dc22

2009016973

ISBN-13: 978-0-8389-1002-3

Printed in the United States of America
13 12 11 10 09 5 4 3 2 1

CONTENTS

ACKNOWLEDGMENTS

The contributors to this guide are generous and talented communicators who have provided their best thinking on a wide array of important topics. They have my gratitude for their contributions and support. I would like to single out Eric Friedenwald-Fishman for his generous contributions and creative insights.

Thanks to my dedicated co-workers John Amundsen, Megan Humphrey, Megan McFarlane, Macey Morales, Jennifer Petersen, and Steve Zalusky.

I also want to thank a number of important people in my life for their encouragement and much more: my mother, Margery Gould, a talented and inspiring artist with the most wonderful outlook on life I have ever encountered; sister Liz Saltzman and her great family, Richard, Carly, Ryan, Isabel, and Sam; my brother Scott Gould; and my sons, Alex and Ben Gould, who inspire me every day of the year. Special thanks to Marla Green for all of her support and assistance. This guide has been prepared in the memory of my father, Morton L. Gould, a man who loved good books, inspired writing, and a lively debate.

INTRODUCTION

Forward-thinking communicators have a lot on their minds these days. Now more than ever, we have to learn to respond quickly to the changing media landscape and our country's demographic shifts in order to develop powerful library and nonprofit sector programs and services. This guide offers the thoughts of experts on many important topics within public relations, plus recommendations and tips on how to use new tools—and some traditional ones—to communicate with your key audiences more effectively.

Reaching diverse and underserved audiences is, in effect, a survival skill for many nonprofit communicators today. This guide offers in-depth chapters on how to reach these growing audiences effectively and how to build public will to cause social change, as well as how the most successful public awareness campaign ever developed for librarians can help your library unify communications through a powerful brand, develop a clearer, stronger voice and more visibility, and amplify your messages through partnerships.

Chapters also cover how to increase library attendance by getting on board the exploding gaming scene, identify key online resources that are useful to communicators in the library world, develop low-cost podcasts for maximum results, and retool some time-tested winners with new twists. This book offers guidance on how to produce successful op-eds, letters to the editor, "state of your library" reports, and public service announcements.

Other chapters discuss how to develop an effective advocacy plan, work with Friends of the Library groups, empower people to deliver your key messages, and more. The rapid changes in the world of daily journalism stand as a metaphor for what is happening in the world of communication more generally. In the past few years, we have all witnessed the growth of online news and a decline in daily newspaper readership. Elizabeth Spayd, editor of washingtonpost.com, says the past few years have seen more radical change in newsrooms than she has ever experienced during her thirty-year career. Douglas Ahlers, a fellow at Harvard University's Kennedy School of Government, says in an article in the *Harvard International Journal of Press/Politics* that executives from the *New York Times* and other newspapers wonder if there will even be a print version of their publications in ten years. Author John Darnton, a forty-year veteran of the *New York Times,* calls newspaper websites "self-inflicted cannibalism" and says that blogs are "the new narrative structure and always subjective." He says the Internet is good at "aggregation, linkage documentation and verification," but that when the truth is not so obvious, bloggers do not dig for it.

In short, this new technological world provides librarians and other nonprofit communicators with myriad opportunities and pitfalls. How all the changes affect our work as communicators should be at the top of our list of concerns as we plan for the future. Online journalism, blogging, reporters with video cameras, podcasts, mobile Internet devices, RSS feeds, interactive graphics—we have to take maximum advantage of all these new channels and devices while maintaining our skills in more traditional media. The goal of this guide is to help you do just that.

INCREASING RELEVANCE, RELATIONSHIPS, AND RESULTS
Principles and Practices for Effective Multicultural Communication

Maria Elena Campisteguy and Eric Friedenwald-Fishman

Every day, thousands of libraries encounter the challenges and the benefits of working in an increasingly multicultural society. From reaching out to potential customers, donors, and taxpayers to providing valuable programs and services, every library in today's society must make effective communication in a multicultural context a key priority. It is an absolute necessity for organizational success and for building healthy communities. Taking a multicultural approach to communication increases the relevance and impact of communication by recognizing, respecting, and engaging the cultural backgrounds of all stakeholders and framing messages in ways that invite real participation and dialogue. Effective multicultural communication unlocks new resources and brings additional perspectives and talents to the table to develop innovative and sustainable solutions to our most challenging social, environmental, and economic issues.

An analysis of the raw data highlights the significance and growth of our nation's increasingly multicultural population. Take ethnicity statistics alone: ethnic and racial groups account for 30 percent of the U.S. population, or more than ninety million people. In 2050, communities of color will make up 49 percent of the U.S. population, or more than 209 million people. Race and ethnicity, however, are not the only indicators of an increasingly diverse population. Currently, there are 41.9 million eighteen- to twenty-nine-year-olds living in America. This figure is more than twice the number of people ages sixty-six to seventy-seven (20.3 million), and represents 21 percent of the overall voting public. These shifts demonstrate the importance of effectively engaging all members of our communities for the success of individual organizations and to ensure an innovative, prosperous, just, and healthy society.

Moving beyond demographics, recent studies highlight a rich mosaic of stereotype-busting interests, priorities, and actions, from buying patterns to charitable giving. Consider this:

In a study done by the Hartman Group, African Americans were found to be 24 percent more likely to be "core" consumers of organic products than their white counterparts.[1] *Core* means they're more dedicated to buying natural products than the mainstream population.

In the business sector, minority- and women-owned businesses have become an influential force, more than twelve million strong and accounting for more than $4 trillion in annual gross sales, according to research from the U.S. Small Business Administration (1999).[2] These businesses represent the fastest-growing areas of the U.S. economy and are responsible for the strongest job creation among all U.S. businesses.

Among the U.S. electorate, Latinos are the fastest-growing ethnic group. Their voter registration and voting rates are growing faster than those of other racial and ethnic groups, according to a 2007 report from the National Council of La Raza.[3]

Network for Good, a major processor of online charitable donations for nonprofits, has reported that online donors tend to be young, with a median age of thirty-eight.[4]

Donors of color are generally motivated to "give back" to the community after achieving success in their own lives, according to a study by the Council on Foundations and the Association of Black Foundation Executives. As reported in the *Chronicle of Philanthropy* (2003), African Americans who give to charity donate 25 percent more of their discretionary income than whites.[5]

Effectively engaging diverse audiences is key to growing and sustaining new customers, ensuring long-term support, increasing philanthropic support, strengthening consumer loyalty, and attracting new volunteers and advocates. Yet many libraries either apply a one-size-fits-all approach to their communication or recognize the need for a multicultural approach but do not know where to start.

At Metropolitan Group, we work with libraries of all types and sizes as well as many leading nonprofit, business, and public sector organizations engaged in multicultural communication and in collaborating with and on behalf of many cultural communities and advocacy organizations. Through our work, we have distilled eight principles for effective multicultural communication. In this chapter, we will provide an overview of each principle. You will see that many of the principles make great sense for communication to all audiences and are built upon well-established communication and social marketing theory. We will also highlight a few practices—tangible actions—to demonstrate how each principle can be applied in a library context. Finally, each principle is illustrated by two examples from work with our clients—one from a library and one from another organization.

The eight principles are

Principle 1. Check Your Assumptions at the Door: *Begin with Yourself*

Principle 2. Understand the Cultural Context(s) of Your Audience: *Do Your Homework*

Principle 3. Invest Before You Request: *Create Community-Centered Partnerships*

Principle 4. Develop Authentic Relationships: *Maintain a Long-Term Perspective*

Principle 5. Build Shared Ownership: *Engage, Don't Just Involve*

Principle 6. Walk Your Talk: *Lead by Example*

Principle 7. Relate, Don't Translate: *Place Communication into Cultural Context*

Principle 8. Anticipate Change: *Be Prepared to Succeed*

We have found these principles and practices to be useful starting points for our work and for our clients' approach to multicultural communication. We hope you will find them to be helpful in your work as well. We also hope they will lead you to discover other effective practices and approaches as you engage with your communities. We know that if your organization is committed to effective multicultural communication and concentrates on building relevance and relationships, you will advance your own goals, achieve results, and increase the social and community capital that benefits us all.

PRINCIPLE 1.
Check Your Assumptions at the Door: Begin with Yourself

Before beginning to work with any group that is culturally, ethnically, or racially different from your own, it is critical to step back and identify any assumptions, preconceived beliefs, or stereotypes that you might hold about that population. Your best intentions may be undermined by old assumptions or isolated experiences that can affect your ability to develop a sound strategy that effectively achieves the behavioral, attitudinal, or systems change you seek. It is also essential that you not assume a particular group holds the same set of values or beliefs as your own.

Recommended Practices

1. *Get the facts.* Often assumptions are based on outdated or incomplete information. At the beginning of any multicultural communication initiative, you should refresh your knowledge by reviewing recent available data on the basic demographics of your audience and its specific behaviors and attitudes in relation to your issue. This can include the audience's purchasing trends, voting patterns, philanthropic contributions, literacy rates, health statistics, etc.

2. *Examine the work of community- and faith-based organizations and programs that serve that cultural group.* Local community-based organizations, or regional and national organizations closely connected to local affiliates that are grounded in your community, are often experts that can be consulted to help evaluate or contribute information, enabling you to establish better understanding and develop more effective communication strategies.

3. *Scan the news media* for articles that demonstrate trends, challenges, and opportunities within and for specific cultural communities. Being familiar with the public discourse issues and perspectives of your audience, and the way these issues and your audience are portrayed in local and national media, helps build your understanding of issues of relevance, insight into community perspectives, and awareness of key players and leaders.

4. *Test your assumptions* through informal discussion groups of five to eight people recruited through your network of contacts; in more formal focus groups with individuals who were recruited according to specific demographic and psychographic data that meet the profile of the audience you want to reach; or by engaging experts from that community. This process helps expose existing beliefs, values, and behaviors within the target audience group early on and provides an opportunity to gain insights into how your audience really views an issue. This step is invaluable in refining strategies and messages, avoiding major pitfalls, and saving costly resources you might otherwise invest in fully developing an outreach strategy that is not valid for your audience.

5. *Check your ego at the door* and approach the work with an open mind, an open heart, and a sense of humor. It is normal for us all to want our work to be successful. However, you should expect that this work will not come about without some multicultural misunderstandings and occasional uneasiness for you or for others who might feel they are out of their comfort zone. Encourage others to provide honest feedback and direction so as to understand where there are cultural differences and how they might affect your communication. Be open to changes in direction and approaches if the original plan does not work.

LIBRARY CASE EXAMPLE:
Center for Puerto Rican Studies at Hunter College (Library and Archives)

ISSUE
Today, there are more than six million Puerto Ricans in the world and nearly half are living in the United States mainland, with one and a half million in the New York tri-state area alone.

The Center for Puerto Rican Studies at Hunter College, also known as Centro de Estudios Puertorriqueños (Centro), is part of City University of New York and is the leading university-based research institute in the United States devoted to the study of the Puerto Rican experience. As Centro neared its thirtieth anniversary, it identified the opportunity to invest in increased archive collection, documentation, and exhibition; to expand its audience base; and to grow its philanthropic support. Yet it did not have an existing culture of marketing and philanthropy or volunteer leadership to champion its cause.

STRATEGY

As Centro launched efforts to establish new marketing outreach programs and recruit advisory committee members and partners, the organization's leadership stepped back and assessed its audience and stakeholders. It identified significant diversity in the Puerto Rican community based upon generation, geography (New York or elsewhere in the United States), and relationship with Puerto Rico's current status (statehood advocates, independence advocates, status quo advocates, etc.). The nature of this diversity and the recognition of varied, yet equally important needs/uses of an archive, educational, and cultural center, guided the development of anniversary programs, marketing materials, and volunteer recruitment that reflected the diverse needs of the community and positioned Centro as a hub with relevance for all.

RESULTS AND IMPACT

Centro's thirtieth anniversary garnered support from business and labor, the public sector, and private funders. It expanded programs, increased participation, and raised awareness across a broad cross section of the community. (See figure 1.1.)

CASE EXAMPLE: "Healthy Birth Initiative"

ISSUE

African American, Latino, Somali, and low-income white women in Portland, Oregon, had disproportionately high rates of infant mortality and low birth-weight babies.[6] County health officials assumed this was because the women were making unhealthy choices (smoking, drinking, drug use, etc.) during pregnancy because they were unaware of the risks to their babies. They planned a public education campaign, "Healthy Birth Initiative," to reach women in these communities.

STRATEGY

Focus groups conducted with women in the target groups proved the initial assumptions wrong. Many pregnant women were aware of the risks, but a lack of support from male partners and friends was a major deterrent to making healthy choices. With this new information, the campaign and message design changed dramatically to include targeted outreach to men. Messages about how to have a healthy pregnancy and a healthy baby were framed using the theme, "What if men could get pregnant?" (See figure 1.2.) Men

FIGURE 1.1 Anniversary campaign brochure celebrating the history, experience, and culture of the Puerto Rican community. By recognizing and reflecting its community's diversity, Centro helped focus its marketing and philanthropy and enhanced its position as a community hub with relevance for all.

were encouraged to provide support to all the pregnant women in their lives. Campaign materials in English and Spanish were distributed in places that men visit, from health clinics to restaurants and barbershops.

RESULTS AND IMPACT

The campaign achieved both behavior and systems change. Infant mortality rates and incidence of low birth weights declined. Male outreach workers were added to the county health team.

PRINCIPLE 2.
Understand the Cultural Context(s) of Your Audience: Do Your Homework

The goal of any communication is creating shared understanding. As communicators, when we relay a

message (language, symbols, images), it is with the expectation that the receiver can interpret it as the sender intended and has the ability to choose to take action accordingly. This is not always the case. Various cultural groups have unique ways of perceiving, organizing, and relating to information. They may have different needs, values, motivators, and behaviors. The norm for one group may not necessarily be relevant or appropriate for another group. The message must fit the cultural context (the norms, ideas, beliefs, and totality of meaning shared by a cultural group) of the audience you want your communication to reach.

The more you learn about the specific communities you want to engage, the more specific and effective your communication and outreach strategies can be.

Recommended Practices

1. *Define your desired audience(s) as specifically as possible.* Major differences often exist within ethnic, racial, and

FIGURE 1.2 Print creative from the "Healthy Birth Initiative" encouraged men to support the women in their lives in having a healthy pregnancy.

cultural groups. Narrowing your focus by evaluating factors such as age, education, reading level, socioeconomic status, ethnicity, geographic area, etc., will help you better analyze the needs, interests, values, concerns, and decision drivers of your audience.

For example, the Asian American, Pacific Islander, and Native Hawaiian population as a broad category is extremely diverse, speaking nearly five hundred languages and dialects and comprising thirty-two different ethnic groups, including Chinese, Japanese, Filipino, Asian Indian, Korean, and Vietnamese. Approaching these populations as one homogenous group would render any strategy completely ineffective. In fact, it could have the opposite effect and generate a negative reaction.

Further, many ethnic and racial communities are made up of people in different stages of acculturation to American society. Some individuals may be recent arrivals to this country or first generation. Others may be second or third generation or may have arrived as children. As a result, they may have very different values, thought processes, decision-making processes, and behavior drivers than those of their parents or grandparents, or even their peers. Cultural influences affect the lens through which people view the world—the way they define their reality, beliefs, and assumptions. Understanding where your audience stands in relation to an issue or desired action, or its attitudes toward a product or service, is key to designing an effective strategy and is a fundamental best practice for all communication.

2. *Be aware of norms, traditions, dialects, and other cultural nuances* that are unique to your audience. Once you have identified your audience, the next step is to begin to understand the characteristics of this cultural group. In addition to consulting any available literature on the demographic and psychographic attributes of your audience, you can revisit the practices outlined under Principle 1 to deepen your understanding of the specific audiences you have identified and prioritized.

Even within a single language group, significant differences in vocabulary and usage must be considered. Although not as diverse a population as the Asian American/Pacific Islander/Native Hawaiian demographic, it can be a mistake—and an ineffective use of resources—to communicate with Hispanics as if they are a homogeneous group. Cultural norms, traditions, and language usage such as slang and colloquialisms vary extensively by Hispanic subpopulation. As suggested in Practice 1 above, you can narrow your focus by evaluating characteristics such as country of origin, length of time in the United States, and level of accul-

turation to help you understand that Latinos may have very different political views, family traditions, use of language, and even attitudes toward public libraries. Although Spanish is the shared language, many words may mean different things to different people depending on the subpopulation. For example, in Puerto Rico a *china* is an orange. *China* in Colombia could refer to a little girl. In many other South American countries a *china* is a Chinese female.

3. *Understand historical experiences and attitudes* that may affect communication. Depending on their age, people may be influenced by different defining moments in history—among them, slavery, the right to vote, the Depression, the civil rights movement, the assassinations of John F. Kennedy and Dr. Martin Luther King Jr., the Columbine High School shootings, the attacks on September 11, and Hurricanes Katrina and Rita.

Ongoing political and legal debates on polarizing issues—such as immigration—are often based on and colored by the unique circumstances of those individuals involved in the discussion. Personal experiences, such as discrimination when seeking housing or credit, can set strong positive or negative perceptions through which people view and respond to organizations, messages, and institutions. For immigrants, there are also relevant home-country events and perceptions that come from personal experience or are shared by relatives who have remained in the home country.

These historical experiences affect how messages are received and how issues, concepts, and organizations are viewed by different cultural groups. For example, first-generation immigrants from former soviet bloc countries have a tendency to distrust financial institutions. They may have experienced state-controlled systems, communities without mortgage lending, bureaucratic regulation that created barriers to small enterprise, and corrupt practices, including bribery, in their home countries. As a result, they may have limited knowledge of financial services such as home mortgages and small business lending. This lack of familiarity and trust must be addressed through education by the right (trusted) messenger and outreach if a bank or community development program is going to attract such customers and serve this community.

Further, literal historical experiences and pop culture references must also be viewed through the lens of a particular community's experience to determine their relevancy and positive or negative impacts as part of a communication strategy. Specific political changes, community victories or injustices, or events such as Woodstock or the grape boycott, can either be effective examples to people who lived through them or absolutely meaningless to those who did not experience them.

4. *Identify and build upon cultural strengths and assets.* When formulating strategies and communication, ensure that they relay a positive message about the targeted audience or highlight assets rather than convey negative stereotypes. Messages can powerfully identify challenges and needs from a strength-based perspective that illustrates an opportunity to meet a need. Such messages will be much better received by your audience and therefore be more effective in bringing about the desired change. Engagement with strategic partners, choice of outreach strategies, and the development of communication tactics that emphasize and build upon cultural strengths can increase trust and more effectively engage desired audiences. (Refer to case example under Principle 7 for an additional example of a social marketing campaign designed to build on the cultural strengths of its audience.)

LIBRARY CASE EXAMPLE:
"Lee y serás" Campaign (an Initiative of the National Council of La Raza, Scholastic Inc., and Verizon)

ISSUE
Currently, 86 percent of Latino fourth-graders and 91 percent of Latino eighth-graders in the United States read at or below basic skill levels. Fewer than 25 percent of Latino seventeen-year-olds can read at the skill level necessary for success in college and the increasingly high-tech workplace. This achievement gap actually begins before children enter kindergarten. A major goal of this national bilingual early-literacy campaign is to empower parents and child care providers to play a first-teacher role.

STRATEGY
As the education system has increasingly encouraged learning English, non-English-speaking parents do not receive encouragement for and may even be discouraged from reading to their children. Also, the traditional message of "read to your children so they will be better prepared for school" does not resonate as well in the Latino community due to a belief by some segments of the community that learning begins in school, not at home. Clearly, traditional literacy frames would not work with this audience. New materials and

a unique creative approach were needed in Spanish *and* developed within a cultural context that the various Latino subpopulations could relate to.

The campaign's focus group research guided the development of a message framework that centered on *succeeding in life*, rather than the dominant literacy frame, "*read to your child so they can succeed in school.*" Latino cultural strengths such as storytelling, rhymes, and singing were emphasized. Further, based upon an understanding of the work-life demands (another cultural context factor) of the primary audience, the message frame highlighted how storytelling and singing could be incorporated into parents' daily activities.

By recognizing that many parents have multiple jobs and cannot meet the demands of traditional messages that call for a set amount of time spent reading each day, the campaign created a culturally relevant frame which was effective with parents and primary caregivers. Six pilot campaign markets were selected to account for cultural needs of specific subpopulations such as Chicanos and Mexican Americans in Los Angeles, Cubans and South Americans in Miami, and Puerto Ricans and Dominicans in New York. Partnerships with preschools, community programs, and libraries delivered content to parents and other care providers.

RESULTS AND IMPACT
Initial impact assessments in the six markets show very promising success. Parents involved in the program clearly and enthusiastically articulate and act on their first-teacher role and articulate the core messages of the campaign in their own words when describing what is important for their children to succeed. Cultural aspects of the program such as rhymes, stories, and songs have been particularly well received. (See figure 1.3.)

CASE EXAMPLE:
National Youth Advocacy Coalition's "You Know Different" Campaign

ISSUE
AIDS is the leading cause of death for people between the ages of fifteen and forty-nine worldwide, and more than 50 percent of new infections each year are among people age twenty-five and younger. The epidemic also disproportionately affects people of color—half of all new HIV infections each year in the United States are among African Americans, and three out of five people living with HIV/AIDS are people of color. Research about youth HIV testing indicated that major barriers

include denial of risk, fear, stigma, misinformation, and lack of relevance of current materials (which usually feature adults). Barriers to testing can be even higher in the African American LGBTQ (lesbian, gay, bisexual, transgender/transsexual or questioning sexuality) community, where males are often "closeted" and unlikely to get tested for fear of rejection by their cultural community.

In 2005, NYAC (National Youth Advocacy Coalition) received a Centers for Disease Control and Prevention grant to increase the rates of HIV testing and test retrieval among African American LGBTQ youth ages thirteen to twenty-four by building capacity among local agencies and conducting a public awareness campaign. The goal of the "You Know Different" campaign was a 100 percent increase in HIV testing and test retrieval in communities engaged in the campaign. The core challenges were to create a campaign that would resonate as authentic and representative with youth in three very different geographic regions, and to create very low-cost, grassroots strategies and tools that would give strategic partners the

FIGURE 1.3 Funded and promoted by the National Council of La Raza, Scholastic Inc., and Verizon, "Lee y serás" was a campaign to support Latino families in helping their children succeed through community-based organizations that have a deep connection with those they serve.

ability to reproduce materials easily and customize them based on their target populations.

STRATEGY

NYAC conducted formative focus groups with the target population to gain more specificity about trusted sources of HIV/AIDS information, how information should be delivered ("by people who look like me"), relevant messages and barriers to seeking HIV testing. Subsequently, research and planning sessions were held with all participating partners in each campaign location, including a group of youths who helped to deepen understanding of the unique cultural needs and capabilities of each community. In addition, a *digital ethnography* process was employed in which participating youths were given digital cameras and asked to "show us who you are." The resulting photographs created the basis for the campaign creative and the clear decision that this campaign would not work utilizing previous creative frames, but needed to use new creative developed specifically for this community.

Initial messages were developed based on the research, and a focus group of youths from each of the test sites evaluated and responded to creative concepts and language. Using an interactive format, messages were finalized with this group. In addition, strategies for reaching youth were tested, and a grassroots network strategy was employed based directly on youth feedback. (See figure 1.4.)

RESULTS AND IMPACT

At the outset of the project, potential partners in the effort envisioned a traditional mass media public awareness campaign. As a result of the strategic approach employed, the campaign approach and creative shifted dramatically toward a youth-centered, youth-driven, grassroots outreach program. The campaign goal of a 100 percent increase in testing and test retrieval was exceeded by 20 percent. Results included

- Number of youths contacting testing organizations increased more than 300 percent.
- Number of HIV tests scheduled increased 220 percent.
- Walk-in testing increased nearly 50 percent.
- HIV tests performed increased 120 percent.

PRINCIPLE 3.
Invest Before You Request: Create Community-Centered Partnerships

Historically, there has been a tendency to reach out to organizations serving special populations at the point when issue advocates, or an institution, need help accessing a community. Too often the first introduction is a request for assistance in conducting outreach, sharing information, facilitating market research, or referring participants to programs. In many cases, communication has been one way and self-centered—what can this person or organization do for us?

Often the request or "offer to help" is framed in a manner that implies a deficiency. Though usually well-intentioned, the approach is easily perceived as "we are here to help you" and/or bring you services or programs that can "correct" the situation.

By investing in the community—learning about organizational needs, attending events and community forums, and participating in community-based efforts—you can build trust and start the foundation for long-term engagement. By taking this step first, before you have a specific programmatic request, you invest in building relationships that lead to long-term partnerships.

Further, by utilizing a strength-based approach—one in which you demonstrate trust in your audience's ability to identify and resolve their own issues—you set the groundwork to build more effective communication and programs that provide mutual benefit and advancement of the mission.

Recommended Practices

1. *Treat leaders, organizations, and community members as partners* with whom you wish to engage, not as a tool for you to use. Don't let the first time a community hears from you be the moment when you want something. Build the relationship from the inside out. Before you ask, give. The creation of community-centered partnerships facilitates the development of long-term relationships.

2. *Learn about a community's needs and assets,* and seek to understand how you can add value. The organizations identified in your early research can be great resources. Quite often they are members of community coalitions and roundtables that meet regularly. Consider attending as a guest to listen to the key issues and concerns that are surfacing in the community that you will be working with. Listen for opportunities to collaborate and share resources.

It is only after you have invested in their work and helped meet their needs that you can ask others to invest in and support your efforts. This is particularly true of communities that have experienced disparities or injustices. Trust must be earned through true willingness to understand the needs and assets of the community and through demonstrating that you want to work collaboratively and invest to add value.

3. *Stay in touch.* Once you establish a new relationship, maintain regular contact through periodic updates, calls, and check-ins so that the relationship remains intact.

FIGURE 1.4 African American LGBTQ youth helped craft messages and define images for this peer-to-peer campaign. A series of images was created for the cities in which the campaign was launched.

LIBRARY CASE EXAMPLE:
North Portland Branch Library

ISSUE

As part of its branch renovation initiative, Multnomah County Library (Oregon) sought to establish neighborhood committees and to garner philanthropic support from residents and businesses to augment public funding for branch renovations and historic restorations and improve furnishings, equipment, and collections. The North Portland branch—a historic Carnegie library located in the city's largest African American neighborhood—presented opportunities to improve programming space on a second floor that was not accessible, improve special collections to serve the community, and restore the beauty and grandeur of the historic building. (See figure 1.5.)

STRATEGY

The library and branch manager had invested in supporting and engaging the community long before the capital campaign. The library had helped establish an educational partnership facilitating collaboration between adjacent high school and community college campuses to offer jointly sponsored programs as well as offer resources to each other's patrons. The library established and invested in special collections, including Black History and Black Literature, as well as expanded collections to serve small business owners. Partnerships with local bookstores, artists, writers, and community leaders established reading, mentorship, and cultural programs to increase youth access to and value for literature, heritage, and the arts. Based upon new and established partnerships, the library and its foundation reached out to leaders from community-based organizations, churches, and businesses and invited their participation in restoring the North Portland branch library by joining an advisory and fund-raising committee. The library made a request based upon a track record of investment.

RESULTS AND IMPACT

Key leaders stepped forward and volunteered to serve on the committee, developed a prospect list, hosted cultivation events, made personal contributions, and solicited contributions from peers. As a result, the community invested in *their* library and in creating an asset to serve their unique local needs. The North Portland branch campaign was the most successful of fourteen branch efforts and resulted in a beautifully restored facility, enhanced funds for collections and programs, and greater community connection and ownership of its neighborhood library.

CASE EXAMPLE:
YMCA of Columbia-Willamette

ISSUE

The YMCA of Columbia-Willamette in Portland, Oregon, was interested in connecting with the fast-growing Latino population in the area. It wanted to increase Latino participation in programs and the number of Latino volunteers and potential donors to the organization.

STRATEGY

The YMCA's president was new to the area, recently relocated from Los Angeles, where he had worked extensively with Latino youth and families. He reached out to a local Latino-led community organization that served children and youth through a variety of programs. He offered transportation, access to facilities, and staff to lead nutrition and fitness classes free of charge.

RESULTS AND IMPACT

The pilot program sparked multiple on-site programs for the Latino organization and joint fund-raising efforts over several years. The organization also gained access to quality facilities, expert staff, and curriculum related to health, fitness, and nutrition to supplement its educational and workforce development programs.

FIGURE 1.5 Images of the North Portland Library (a branch of Multnomah County Library), a historic Carnegie library located in North Portland, Oregon's largest African American neighborhood.

Hundreds of children and teens benefited from year-round health and fitness programming. (See figure 1.6.) Over time, this relationship led to new Latino board members, an increase in Latino volunteers, and an increase in the number of Latino youths and families attending YMCA programs and services—the original goal.

PRINCIPLE 4.
Develop Authentic Relationships: Maintain a Long-Term Perspective

Authentic relationships are those that engage community members in idea generation, feedback, and decision making. Such a relationship is patiently developed because there is no need to rush to get to know and understand each other. The relationship is based on a true sense of shared values and shared mission and is focused on ongoing collaboration rather than a specific project. Communication, contribution, and commitment are all two-way.

Recommended Practices

1. *Go to the community.* Don't expect community members to come to you until they know and trust you. You can build that trust by regularly attending events and visiting venues that are important to the community. Depending on the issue and geographic scope, events and venues can include community fairs, community centers, schools, universities, markets, places of worship, civic clubs, and conferences and special events (local, regional, or national).

2. *Work with trusted allies.* These are individuals and organizations that already have a relationship with members of the community and can help open doors and introduce you. Building relationships with trusted allies is an excellent investment of time and resources.

3. *Don't become a "one-hit wonder,"* getting what you need and never coming back. Commit to the long term and take the initiative to follow up after completion of programs or initiatives to seek further collaboration and to understand where you can contribute to other priorities in the community.

4. *Become an ally.* Be supportive as issues important to the community come up, even if those issues are not always at the top of your own list of priorities. There is a critical role that individuals from outside a cultural group can play as effective and knowledgeable facilita-

tors and advocates for change within a specific community.

A great example of this principle goes back a few years, when a wave of anti-immigrant measures that originated in California appeared to take root in Oregon. Immediately, Basic Rights Oregon, the state's chief advocacy, education, and political organization working to end discrimination based on sexual orientation and gender identity, reached out to PCUN, an Oregon union of farm, nursery, and reforestation workers, which was also the state's largest Latino organization. Basic Rights Oregon offered its support as an ally in the fight against discrimination, including resources and research about what Oregonians thought of discrimination.

LIBRARY CASE EXAMPLE:
Multnomah County Library

ISSUE
Through detailed tracking of who participates in Multnomah County Library's Summer Reading Program, the library's children's services staff could see exactly which child care centers were or were not participating in the program. They observed that the majority of

FIGURE 1.6 The YMCA of Columbia-Willamette reached out to a local Latino-led, community-based organization and offered transportation, facilities, and staff for free fitness and nutrition programs, building relationships that resulted in Latino participation on the YMCA's board and in programs.

Slavic-language community centers were not responding to English-language promotional materials. (See figure 1.7.)

STRATEGY

Using very limited resources, the library brought in a Russian-speaking part-time outreach assistant from a community agency to create connections through phone calls and personal visits that would help Slavic-language community centers understand, trust, and eventually utilize library services. It took repeated messages of what the library is, what the library can provide, and why reading success is important for youth in order to gain access to this population. The outreach specialist started with phone calls (conducted in Russian) and then made in-person visits to the centers and home child care facilities. She also provided story time for the children and coached staff about library resources. Through the relationships built—community center by community center—enrollment in the Summer Reading program increased. The outreach specialist also signed up dozens of new sites for the book delivery service, helping extend the service beyond Summer Reading into year-round participation with the library.

RESULTS AND IMPACT

As a result of this relationship building, Slavic-language community centers began to participate not only in the Summer Reading program, but also began to take advantage of the library's book delivery service.

"We've found it to be true for many cross-cultural relationships that before engaging people in library services, we must create a dialogue of trust in order to reach target populations," says Katie O'Dell, school-age services manager, Multnomah County Library.

CASE EXAMPLE:
New Seasons Market

ISSUE

New Seasons Market is a chain of Oregon grocery stores committed to building strong communities and supporting a healthy regional food economy and environment. Unlike many stores that carry a similar array of natural and organic foods, New Seasons has opened several stores in underserved neighborhoods that include the established African American community, a growing Latino population, and many new Southeast Asian and Eastern European immigrants;

these stores are in locations that were abandoned by traditional grocers decades ago. New Seasons needed to establish community support to build the stores and a strong customer base in neighborhoods that other grocers had considered unprofitable.

STRATEGY

New Seasons' CEO and other leaders began attending neighborhood meetings prior to placing new stores. They learned from community members that a major need and priority was bringing a grocery store with healthy food into the neighborhood. They garnered community feedback on store location, product mix, and service needs. They began hiring and recruiting from the neighborhood for jobs in their other stores while new stores were in development. They participated in priority neighborhood projects from street tree plantings to sponsoring a youth entrepreneurship program at one store site. They advocated as an ally of the community for improved transit and other needs.

RESULTS AND IMPACT

New Seasons opened two large stores in neighborhoods without a grocery store and hired staff at all levels that reflected the local community. The diverse customer base from the neighborhoods has made both stores very successful. (See figure 1.8.) New Seasons has forged strong community partnerships

FIGURE 1.7 Summer reading collateral developed to support statewide outreach to children and families from various backgrounds and geographic regions.

and relationships, providing it with allies on priority issues of food policy. In turn, New Seasons has been engaged as an ally for community development and economic equity priorities. Further, local communities have pointed to New Seasons as an example of the expectation they have for other companies that benefit from doing business in their neighborhood.

PRINCIPLE 5. Build Shared Ownership: Engage, Don't Just Involve

As you seek to engage the community in your work, look for opportunities for the community to become vested in the mission that drives your work and its outcomes. Identify opportunities for leadership roles for members of the community and engage them as decision makers and owners of strategy. Actively seek their guidance and input in evaluating and refining strategies and messages. When there is more than one cultural group that you wish to engage, identify the needs, values, and motivators that the groups have in common and use these to develop messages and strategies that help unify the groups. This approach helps build community, ensures that groups do not feel they are in competition for attention or resources, and also helps to identify and elevate shared community needs and values that help shape ongoing dialogue.

The possibilities for bringing people together can be as creative as you wish and will differ depending upon the program, needs, and specific communities. Regardless of the format, ensure that your efforts are not superficially involving people for the sake of being able to say that input was received from community members. Rather, listen to and act upon advice and build programs where all partners describe them as *ours* and ask how *we* are going to succeed. Your response and feedback to their input will be critical in building credibility, trust, and ownership among community members.

FIGURE 1.8 New Seasons Market invests in community before opening new stores, garnering input from the community, hiring from the community, and being an advocate for key community needs, from public transit to street trees.

Recommended Practices

1. *Make sure there are seats at the table.* Develop input and decision-making structures that demonstrate and reinforce ownership. This engagement may take many forms, depending upon the project and communities. Whether ownership is built as a coalition, a steering committee, an advisory group, board-level counsel, or a working group, the shared responsibility the process creates will result in much more effective and successful multicultural communication.

For example, when CentroNía, a Washington, D.C.–based provider of bilingual and multicultural educational programs and family-support services for children from birth to age eighteen, needed a new brand, its process included hiring four teenagers from the center to work alongside writers and designers.[7] The youths had "grown up" at the center; some had been there since their toddler years.

As part of the project, a Branding 101 course provided training for the students and, at the same time, provided the opportunity for them to teach the branding professionals about *their* organization. The result was a new brand that truly resonates with the African American and Latino communities the organization serves.

2. *Establish shared decision making and shared authority.* Build coalitions and partnerships with groups from your target audiences. Identify protocols for participation

and decision making as well as for the joint development and facilitation of agendas and meetings.

3. *Engage partners as adaptors, not adopters.* Learn from the field and incorporate what you learn into communication program design and execution. Build feedback and testing sessions into overall strategies and allow time to make refinements based on that feedback. When Washington County (Oregon) developed its twenty-year strategic plan, all of the diverse communities that make the county their home were invited to participate through a series of community forums, discussion groups, and other opportunities for input. Farmers, high-tech professionals, retired seniors, Koreans, Hispanic migrant workers, and youth were among the populations that were actively sought out and engaged in developing and refining the plan. These seemingly disparate audiences had unifying needs and motivators. They shared an appreciation of and a commitment to the county where they lived and worked. They all had a common interest in ensuring a safe, clean, and sustainable environment that promised quality of life for them and their families.

LIBRARY CASE EXAMPLE:
King County Library System

ISSUE
After more than forty years of public support, King County Library System (KCLS) in Washington State experienced its first bond measure defeat in 2002. In 2003, KCLS decided to place a $172 million capital replacement bond before voters on the fall 2004 ballot. The goal was to create an environment in which KCLS has the capital resources needed to ensure a continued level of quality service to the King County region for the next ten years.

STRATEGY
KCLS developed and implemented a robust community visioning, listening, and outreach program to learn from patrons what was most important to them in their libraries. Following these sessions, library staff actively shared what they learned in reports back to the community. Based on what they learned, they developed a public information program to educate library patrons about the fall 2004 bond measure. The library's core strategy was driven by the values defined by the community related to library services and facilities, and the development of key message themes that were also driven by community values. KCLS also focused its work on strengthening internal capacity through

training of library staff, and design of public outreach tools and key tactics for staff use in educating the public about the bond measure.

The library system faced a unique set of challenges because it's located in the same county as Seattle, the state's largest city. Seattle has its own library system (Seattle Public Library), which had recently passed a public funding measure and was completing construction of a new central facility. The major media of the region are located in Seattle, and there is significant voter confusion about the two systems despite their serving very different urban/suburban markets.

RESULTS AND IMPACT
With limited financial resources and strong leveraging of the library's core assets—its people—the KCLS education initiative resulted in overwhelming success.

King County Library reached out to more than 175 gatherings of community members and garnered broad support from library patrons, numerous cities, and chambers of commerce throughout King County. (See figure 1.9.) As a public agency, the library was appropriately focused on patron education and outreach. A private political action committee, People for Libraries, was convened and leveraged the strategy and messaging of the education campaign, raising about $125,000 to promote passage of the bond measure. The bond passed with 63 percent of the vote, and the education work conducted has been leveraged in the several years after bond passage to ensure appropriate input on the design and programming of more than twenty new or renovated libraries throughout the system. This strong

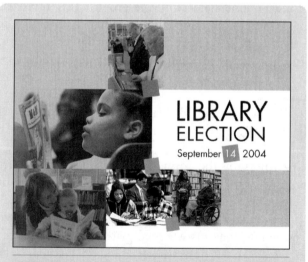

FIGURE 1.9 Education collateral that expresses the King County Library System's core strategy and messages, which were developed based on the community's closely held values.

level of community ownership is a hallmark of the library's exceptional programs and services.

KCLS was awarded the Public Relations Society of America's national Silver Anvil Award of Excellence in Public Affairs for this work.

CASE EXAMPLE:
National Lewis and Clark Bicentennial

ISSUE
The National Lewis and Clark Bicentennial commemoration was being planned in the shadow of the controversial 500th anniversary of Christopher Columbus's arrival in America. The latter event was perceived by many as divisive—as celebrating the beginnings of destructive impacts on Native Americans and perpetuating a myopic narrative that dismissed thousands of years of history and culture. To engage people in an important historical commemoration with relevance to all Americans, a very different approach was required.

STRATEGY
From the start, the descendants of the tribes and bands that explorers Lewis and Clark encountered were part of a national coalition formed to determine the goals, vision, and strategy of the bicentennial. The coalition decided that the point of the commemoration should not be to tell Lewis and Clark's story, but rather to tell many stories through the diverse perspectives of this historic journey and the impact it had on all peoples.

Three themes emerged for the commemoration: understanding intercultural perspectives, understanding environmental stewardship, and understanding the importance of learning. The governing board of the coalition included many tribal leaders. A broader advisory board and independent programming organization, the Circle of Tribal Advisors, was established with leadership from thirty-eight federally recognized tribes. Program exhibits, thirteen national signature events, and a national ad campaign—all speaking from diverse perspectives—told a more powerful story.

RESULTS AND IMPACT
The decision to commemorate, not to celebrate, and to tell stories of mutual learning and impacts (positive and negative)

created a national dialogue that built connections and increased understanding. It also created an extremely successful national program, garnering the participation of millions of Americans and massive media coverage that exceeded goals and is seen as a benchmark model for historic commemorations. (See figure 1.10.) Further, it drove lasting changes in curriculum, exhibits, commemorative signs, and programs that changed the Lewis and Clark narrative and created strong connections to current issues of environmental stewardship and tribal sovereignty.

PRINCIPLE 6.
Walk Your Talk: Lead by Example

All of us have had experiences in which the message conveyed by an organization is inconsistent with its actions and behaviors. The classic example is a retail business with a huge welcome sign in the window and a staff that ignores you; this is just a manifestation of the challenges audiences experience when the message doesn't match the experience.

If you say that your programs are flexible, open to all members of the community, and based on community needs, then that must be what your audience experiences. If you commit to collaboration, then you must behave collaboratively. If you are committed to providing services to *everyone* in the community, then your organization's staff, governance, and partnerships need to reflect the community, and your resources need to benefit that community. Anything short of this tells the audiences you wish to engage with that you're not authentic. It raises suspicion and erodes the

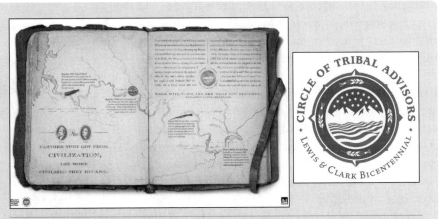

FIGURE 1.10 "The farther they got from civilization, the more civilized they became" (from an ad promoting the Circle of Tribal Advisors awareness campaign).

foundation for trust. As discussed in Principle 5, the practices below are not limited to working with one cultural group at a time and can be applied to multiple audiences.

Recommended Practices

1. *Acknowledge the reality of your organization.* Conduct a self-assessment: Examine who your organizational policy makers, decision makers, and program or department managers are. Do they reflect the community in which you live and the customers you serve? Who are your donors? Have you diversified your base of support? Do the communities you serve also have the opportunity to reciprocate by investing in your work? If your organization does not reflect the diversity of the audiences you are hoping to engage, be transparent about your efforts and challenges. For most organizations, this is a journey. Clarity about your particular journey and real investments create a foundation for trust and collaboration.

2. *Do what you say you believe others should do.* When you set goals to broaden your reach and communicate internally about the importance of tapping into new markets or reaching new populations, make sure you are aligning your own organization's operations with your goals. Do your programs, products, or services align with the cultural values and serve the needs of your diverse stakeholders? When you publicly espouse the value of embracing new and emerging communities, do your internal actions reflect these words? Are your governance structure, policies, and staffing reflective of your vision?

Once you conduct your self-assessment, be diligent about creating a measurable and actionable plan that addresses the areas where you have fallen short. Your assessment should serve as a blueprint for how your organization will take action to better reflect the community that you serve and strengthen your multicultural communication competency.

3. *Deliver on promises.* Recognize that commitments made to partner organizations, customers, and donors are important with all audiences, and many multicultural groups may even hold you to a higher standard. As discussed above, historical experiences and current experiences of disparities create barriers to trust. A broken promise will be seen as a nearly unforgivable breach of confidence.

To ensure that promises build faith and trust, make sure they are communicated clearly in diverse media (in person and in writing). Engage others in your organization and in the community you are working with to share the promise. Establish regular check-ins or other methods to ensure frequent communication when needed adjustments and changes can be mutually determined rather than turning into real or perceived broken promises.

LIBRARY CASE EXAMPLE: West Hollywood Library ("Like No Other" Campaign)

ISSUE

West Hollywood, a creative and culturally diverse community, has outgrown its small library built in 1959. The city was established in November 1984 through the grassroots work of affordable housing advocates and members of the LGBTQ (lesbian, gay, bisexual, transgender/transsexual, or questioning sexuality) community to establish a city with affordable housing, respect for all residents, and high quality of life. Today, West Hollywood has one of the largest lesbian, gay, transgender/transsexual communities in the country (more than one-third of adult residents, according to a 2002 City of West Hollywood Human Services Department report),[8] a large Russian immigrant community, and a growing Hispanic community. The city is densely populated, with very little community or civic space and extremely limited open space.

STRATEGY

The city of West Hollywood developed a plan for a new library that would keep the promise of a welcoming community with high quality of life for all residents. The plan relocates the library and includes a parking structure to replace large surface parking lots, while nearly doubling open green space in one of the city's only parks. The library design includes a large com-

FIGURE 1.11 The design of the new West Hollywood library includes a gay and lesbian collection and archive, an HIV/AIDS resource center, and other services that reflect the specific needs and exciting culture of West Hollywood.

munity space for public meetings, presentations, cultural programs, and exhibits; an HIV/AIDS resource center; special collections for LGBTQ literature and archives; Russian and Spanish language collections; and a job/career resource center.

RESULTS AND IMPACT

The city established its first significant public-private partnership to invest $40 million in public funding for the new library and develop a $10 million philanthropic campaign. (See figure 1.11.) Community leaders established a library foundation committed to garnering support for the campaign and ongoing support for unique programs and services designed to meet specific community needs. The foundation's leadership represents a cross section of residents, business leaders, and civic leaders. The campaign has garnered early leadership support and is ahead of schedule, with the new library projected to open in fall 2011.

CASE EXAMPLE:
The Saint Paul Foundation

ISSUE

As the population of racial and ethnic minorities rapidly increased, the city and surrounding suburbs of St. Paul, Minnesota, began experiencing racial tensions. The Saint Paul Foundation is one of the largest community foundations in the country and a long-time community leader in its region. The foundation recognized that a critical need in the community was to advance antiracism efforts.

STRATEGY

After the foundation identified antiracism as a major priority, it reviewed its grant-making program and found disparities throughout the process. It made those disparities known and began a long-term commitment to revise programs and track results. The foundation then commissioned deep community research on attitudes and behaviors concerning race and racism and developed "Facing Race: We're All in This Together," a community outreach initiative to engage others in building an antiracist community. (See figure 1.12.) At the initiative's launch, a speech by the foundation's president included an assessment of the organization's own diversity needs (board/staff diversity and multicultural training). She publicly made a commitment to address these needs, acknowledged that the road ahead would be bumpy, and highlighted the need for open communication and action.

FIGURE 1.12 The Saint Paul Foundation developed a tool to help community members engage in dialogue on race and walked its talk by focusing on its own needs and challenges as it engaged the community.

RESULTS AND IMPACT

The foundation has increased the diversity of its staff and has brought a multicultural perspective to the forefront of all board discourse, conducted an internal climate assessment, provided training to staff, and increased grant-making to community-based organizations in communities of color. Along the way, the foundation has experienced many successes and a few challenges with staff transitions and program communication. The foundation addressed the challenges by working with community members to provide feedback and find solutions.

PRINCIPLE 7.
Relate, Don't Translate: Place Communication into Cultural Context

Successful multicultural communication requires more than just translating English-language content. It requires embracing the social nuances of diverse cultural groups and markets and actively engaging them in the creation of relevant communication strategies, tools, and messages that have the best opportunity to achieve the desired action. When existing strategies are deemed effective, the process of adaptation for new audiences is much broader than the words on a page. In fact, more important than which language to use in your materials is ensuring that the content resonates with the culture and identity of your audience.

Effective multicultural communication takes into account how people from a unique cultural, ethnic, or racial group will interpret your messages, verbal or nonverbal. It entails appropriate interpersonal communication dynamics, the right context, and appropriate usage of culturally relevant imagery, vocabulary, vernacular, metaphors, or slang. Translation makes things readable, not necessarily relevant. A better approach is to make a conscious choice between translating existing concepts that work, relating existing concepts into new images and words that convey ideas more effectively, or developing completely new creative (message frame, copy, imagery).

Recommended Practices

1. *Determine if existing creative works for the audience* and is based on cultural context. Review existing creative with advisors from the priority community and evaluate it against the cultural context information you have gathered through your project planning. Can the core creative concept work with simple translation into other languages? Can it be adapted to be a better cultural fit for your audience, or does new creative need to be developed? If the existing creative works, follow translation protocols to ensure quality. (See practice 4 below.) Critical to this process is upfront identification of the desired behavior you want from your audience.

2. *Relate the existing concept to the needs of your priority audience.* If the existing creative idea works but the execution (images and copy) does not translate in ways that are meaningful to your audience, rework the creative by selecting new images and writing new copy that convey the core idea in the language and cultural context of your audience.

3. *Develop new creative.* If the core idea in existing creative approaches does not work as a translation or as a reworking, developing stand-alone creative that connects with the values, is relevant to the cultural context, and meets the needs of your primary audience

is far more cost-effective than investing in translations that do not work or can send negative messages. Remember, when developing, testing, or adapting new creative, engage your audience and build ownership using methods discussed in Principles 2 and 5.

4. *Establish clear translation protocols.* To ensure high-quality translations that accurately convey your message, hire qualified, certified translators who are translating into their native language. Use a separate, independent, equally qualified reader to review the translation. Provide as much information and context as possible to both translators so they understand your audience, particularly in terms of subpopulation, age, reading levels, and goals of the translated piece. Translated copy being laid out by a graphic designer should go through an additional round of review prior to going to print. Remember, your translation is a reflection of your organization. You should put as much care into it as you would when preparing and finalizing English-language materials.

5. *Don't forget to implement.* Translation does not equal dissemination. Quite often organizations use translations or new creative as an end goal and forget to think through the outreach and dissemination strategy. What happens when someone responds to your communication? Is there someone who speaks the language on the other end to respond? If materials aimed at a mainstream audience are translated and include reference to a website, are there linkages and information connected to that site that will support the desired call to action? Is the content on the site translated? Think through the life cycle of any communication from the point of view of your primary audience and ensure that at each point they can easily get what they need.

LIBRARY CASE EXAMPLE: American Library Association ("en tu biblioteca")

ISSUE

With a population of 44 million, Latinos are the fastest-growing ethnic group in the United States. However, Latinos are less likely than any population group to take full advantage of the resources, services, and materials available through their libraries. A study released in 2008 by the American Library Association reported that while 63 percent of whites and 64 percent of African Americans visited their public libraries in 2006, less than half of Latinos (49 percent) did so.

This results in an *opportunity gap* in a wide range of areas, including health, entrepreneurship, home ownership, employment, early literacy and education, finances, travel, law, citizenship, language, and culture. The impact of this gap is felt in all communities—in lower rates of literacy and school achievement, lower job earnings, greater health challenges, etc.

The "en tu biblioteca" campaign was planned to increase Latino communities' recognition, perceived value and use of the resources available through their libraries, and the opportunities presented to them and their families by these resources.

STRATEGY

ALA was determined to build upon its successful @ your library campaign with a focused campaign to increase Latino use of libraries. The goal of this new campaign, titled "en tu biblioteca," is to help close the opportunity gap for Latino communities through increased awareness, perceived value, and use of library resources.

When it was time to develop the creative for the campaign, ALA reviewed its existing creative and its research on Latino community needs and values, and then analyzed the message framing. Based upon this analysis, ALA decided to create new messaging and campaign creative rather than translate existing materials. This decision recognized the value of providing increased focus on specific areas where libraries could help meet high-priority needs and opportunities and emphasized the invitation libraries can make to the community and the message that librarians are here to help. The campaign ads and materials were designed in Spanish first and then translated into English. (See figure 1.13.)

RESULTS AND IMPACT

Libraries in the twenty communities with the largest Latino populations have committed to the campaign, and the leading Spanish-language radio network and most popular Spanish-language website—Univision— has committed to partnering on the campaign as a media sponsor.

CASE EXAMPLE:
National Resource Center on Diversity for End-of-Life Care

ISSUE

Traditionally, conversations about planning for end-of-life care within communities of color have been

FIGURE 1.13 Redesigned creative for "en tu biblioteca," ALA's largest-ever bilingual advertising campaign seeking to close the "opportunity gap" by promoting library usage in Latino communities.

difficult or nonexistent among family members and/ or health care providers. The topic demands communication that crosses cultural divides and the ability for providers to meet the needs of patients and family members in ways that may differ from those of the mainstream population.

STRATEGY

The National Resource Center on Diversity in End-of-Life Care, coordinated by ALTA Consulting Group, a Washington, D.C.–based African American– and Hispanic-owned company, wanted to develop a Spanish-language compendium of national resources for end-of-life care and recognized that a specific approach would be needed.

In contrast to the English-language version, illustrated in black and white with serene images of trees and landscapes, the Spanish version, it was decided, would feature large, bold photographs of people across many generations. The tone of the content and introductory language would emphasize relationships and the importance of family-based decisions for end-of-life care. Images would be emphasized with bold red and cream colors. (See figure 1.14.)

RESULTS AND IMPACT

The culturally specific design and content received an overwhelmingly positive response from community-

FIGURE 1.14 The design and copywriting approach for photos, colors, tone, and content of the Spanish-language compendium (the cover of which is included here) was culturally specific.

based, statewide, and national organizations that work to promote quality end-of-life care.

PRINCIPLE 8.
Anticipate Change: Be Prepared to Succeed

If done correctly, over time the application of a multicultural perspective to an organization's communication and work creates organizational change. Organizations move from a monocultural perspective that does not acknowledge differences to one that values, utilizes, and engages diverse perspectives. This change occurs not just at the personal level (beliefs and attitudes of individuals) and interpersonal level (how individuals in the organization communicate with each other and with stakeholders), but also at institutional (policies, procedures) and cultural (organizational norms, expectations) levels.

Bringing new people into your organization, especially those from a cultural group that has not been previously engaged—be they staff, volunteers, customers, donors, or community partners—will naturally change the dynamics of your organization. It may change how the organization is structured, governed, and staffed. It may affect how consensus is built, how meetings are managed, and how decisions are made. It may influence how a product is reformulated or how a marketing campaign is planned and executed. When conducting multicultural communication, answer the questions: "Are we prepared to succeed?" "Are we ready for change?"

Recommended Practices

1. *Recognize that your process and approach to the work may change.* Traditional ways of working within an organization may change, based on having new people at the table who may hold a different worldview than your own. They may bring different ways of thinking and may have different needs for discussing and processing information. For example, in Native American communities, the need to process information and hold several conversations before driving for a decision is very important. This is how authentic relationships and trust are built. To drive through an agenda with new information and immediately push to a decision would create distrust and distress. Embrace the change and see the value in new approaches. Be patient with the change process. Don't be afraid to ask for feedback from community members or to ask lots of questions.

2. *Continue to build infrastructure to support multicultural success.* As your programs, initiatives, and organization change, it will be critical to support the changes with intentional recruitment, retention, and training, and capacity building for staff and board members. Consider adopting organizational policies that publicly commit to and support a multicultural environment. In addition, it is important to strengthen internal and external communication programs to regularly update stakeholders and to document new ways of operating, learning, community feedback, impact, and results. The investment of resources to support infrastructure for a multicultural environment will provide strong returns in increased relevance and impact.

LIBRARY CASE EXAMPLE:
Association of Research Libraries

ISSUE

The Association of Research Libraries (ARL) recognized the importance of diversifying the field to reflect the communities it serves. As a generation of library leadership prepares to retire and MLS program students still do not reflect the diversity of America, the field has a challenge and opportunity to recruit a more multicultural pool of candidates to the profession.

STRATEGY

ARL leadership established diversity recruitment to the profession as a core long-term priority and established specific programs (scholarships for MLS programs, conference participation, and training), a member-driven committee, and dedicated staff to sup-

FIGURE 1.15 Recognizing the importance of diversifying the field to reflect the communities it serves, the Association of Research Libraries (ARL) established diversity recruitment as a core long-term priority and established specific programs and dedicated staff to support its effort.

port this effort. ARL's members recognized that they needed to demonstrate that this was a priority issue and they agreed to contribute additional resources on an annual basis beyond dues to support the effort. Furthermore, ARL leadership identified that change needed to occur at all levels of the profession and that specific work was needed to support more diverse participation in management and leadership to create environments in libraries that would achieve their goals. They developed a fellows program to support emerging leaders with mentorships and other experiences that would prepare and position them for leadership roles in research libraries.

RESULTS AND IMPACT

The ARL scholarships have successfully supported highly qualified students of color enrolling in and graduating from MLS programs, have diversified participation at ARL conferences, and are helping diversify the pool of professionals entering the field. (See figure 1.15.) The leadership fellows program has been fully subscribed and has received excellent evaluations; its graduates are being promoted and hired into positions of leadership and are engaged in outreach and support of ARL diversity efforts.

CASE EXAMPLE:
National Assembly on School-Based Health Care

ISSUE

In 2004, the National Assembly on School-Based Health Care (NASBHC) committed to applying a multicultural perspective to its work at all levels of the organization. This included authentic engagement with the communities that the organization and its member affiliates serve. These populations include communities of color and youth. The organization had struggled in the past with how to include youths at its annual convention in a way that was healthy, safe, and meaningful for them and for adult participants.

STRATEGY

The staff and board members attended multicultural development training as a team. This enabled them to establish a common vocabulary and mutually agreed upon guidelines for discussing and celebrating cultural differences among the staff and membership. The opportunity gave them a consciousness about multiculturalism that now plays out much more intentionally in the public face of the organization (website images, speakers, staff, board, etc.). They looked at staff and board composition, studied annual conference workshops and presenters, and recruited a diverse committee to review all communication materials to assess and improve application of a multicultural lens.

Additionally, one staff person's time was shifted to focus on youth engagement at the national convention and to identify opportunities for authentic youth engagement within the organization, such as a youth advisory board. The 2008 convention marked the first time the organization incorporated a comprehensive youth track planned by young people. Several teams of youths from around the country were invited as presenters. The organization offered partial scholarships to encourage youth participation.

NASBHC is currently establishing relationships with community- and faith-based organizations with youth constituents and developing a plan to reach out to other strategic partners. Once every quarter, the staff comes together for frank discussions about disparities relating to oppression. The executive director carries with him guidelines for successful multicultural communication, and those guidelines are integrated into all internal and external meetings and posted in the organization's conference room.

RESULTS AND IMPACT

The organization now has a more diverse staff and board of directors, and hundreds of youths are being engaged in its work and in the work of its affiliates. (See figure 1.16.) Communication tools have been revised to more accurately reflect the organization and its constituents. Many of the affiliates have also attended intensive multicultural development training and are identifying and implementing opportunities for applying a multicultural lens to their policy and advocacy work.

FIGURE 1.16 The National Assembly on School-Based Health Care (NASBHC) made a commitment to engage all the diverse communities the organization and its affiliates serve and identified youth engagement as an area of challenge.

Conclusion

Effective multicultural communication is a critical factor in engaging and garnering support from the full spectrum of voters, donors, advocates, constituents, and stakeholders that make up the American mosaic. By applying the eight principles and their accompanying practices, your library can better advance your goals and mission and help create a stronger and more equitable society. While there are many nuances, approaches, and perspectives to learn and apply, ultimately it all comes down to what we like to call the three Rs: relevance, relationships, and results.

Please feel free to share this material with others, to model this approach, and to speak out as a champion for the increased understanding and engagement that result from effective multicultural communication.

Notes

The authors thank the following Metropolitan Group executives for their contributions to this chapter: Laura K. Lee Dellinger, Brian Detman, and Jennifer Gilstrap Hearn.

1. The Hartman Group, *Organic 2006: Consumer Attitudes and Behavior, Five Years Later and Into the Future,* www.hartman-group.com/publications/reports/organic-2006-consumer-attitudes-behavior-five-years-later-into-the-future.

2. Ron Wesson, "Growth of minority- and women-owned business segment leads to new marketing purchasing opportunities," *Business Credit,* October 1, 1999. www.allbusiness.com/specialty-businesses/women-owned-businesses/334053-1.html.

3. Lindsay Daniels and Clarissa Martinez De Castro, *The Latino Electorate: Profile and Trends* (Washington, DC: National Council of La Raza, 2007).

4. Network for Good, "The Young and the Generous: A Study of $100 Million in Online Giving to 23,000 Charities" (Bethesda, MD: Network for Good, 2008). http://artsandsciences.virginia.edu/kipps/documents/NFG100MillionStudy.pdf.

5. Cited in Association of Baltimore Area Grantmakers, "The New Landscape in Philanthropic Giving." www.abagmd.org/info-url2444/info-url_show.htm?doc_id=484188.

6. The terms *Latino* and *Hispanic* are used interchangeably throughout this chapter to refer to persons of Cuban, Central and South American, Dominican, Mexican, Puerto Rican, Spanish, and other Hispanic descent; they may be of any race. Both terms are used by the U.S. Census Bureau.

7. As part of the rebrand, CentroNía's name was derived from the universal language of Esperanto (*centro* means center, *nía* means our) and Swahili (*nia* means purpose). www.centronia.org.

8. Sara Kocher Consulting, "City of West Hollywood Demographic Profile 2002," prepared for the Human Services Department; available at www.weho.org/download/index.cfm/fuseaction/DetailGroup/navid/159/cid/1666/.

2

BUILDING PUBLIC WILL FOR LIBRARIES

Eric Friedenwald-Fishman and Laura K. Lee Dellinger

After three decades of litigation against tobacco companies with little change in public perception about smoking, the tobacco industry now pays billions for public health programs, smoke-free public spaces are the norm, and smoke-free restaurants and hotels are in high demand from consumers. What changed? Public will.

For years, Detroit insisted that it could not produce hybrid vehicles affordably, and that even if it could, there would be no market for the product. In 2004, Americans were putting their names on waiting lists and paying above list price to buy hybrids. In 2005, luxury cars joined the hybrid mix. What changed? Public will.

Twenty-five years ago, organic agricultural products were found exclusively in natural food stores. Today, organic food drives a $16 billion industry, and can be found on the shelves of every major grocery store across the country. What changed? Public will.

In the late 1990s, Multnomah County Library's Central Library was deemed unsafe, with many areas off limits to the public. It could have become a symbol for a declining system, but it didn't. What changed? Public will.

Over the years, Portland, Oregon's Multnomah County Library made an integrated effort to learn what customers valued, to connect to those values, and to communicate the value the library delivers with frequency and consistency. In the process, it fostered a high level of personal conviction throughout the thriving metropolitan area that the library is a vital resource. For eighteen years the library has provided residents with numerous opportunities to take action based on that conviction—to express their will for the library to flourish.

Communication that fuels lasting change and creates sticking power for an issue, idea, or point of view is a critical and powerful tool for social change, whether aimed at pushing or supporting decision makers to change policy; altering the voting, buying, or other behavior patterns of private citizens; or triggering a change in the economic, political, or social expectations of society.

Public will building is a communication approach that has developed organically through practical experience in social-change-focused communication campaigns conducted by the authors. For more than a decade, Metropolitan Group has been engaged by numerous public sector, nonprofit, and socially responsible business clients to develop communication campaigns to affect attitudes and behaviors and to ultimately create social change. Often, the issues we are engaged in require long-term commitment and reinforcement for the change to last. Through our work we have learned and refined effective approaches that establish platforms for more sustainable change. We have distilled our experience with this work into a communication framework and underlying principles we have named *public will building*.

This chapter shares our learning; defines public will building; creates an understanding of the differences between this approach and public opinion-based communication; highlights the five phases of public will building; and explores the techniques it uses.

Defining Public Will

Public will building is a communication approach that builds public support for social change by integrating grassroots outreach methods with traditional mass media tools in a process that connects an issue to the existing, closely held values of individuals and groups. This approach leads to deeper public understanding and ownership of social change. It creates new and lasting community expectations that shape the way people act, think, and behave.

Public will building

- connects people to an issue through their values, rather than trying to change those values
- results in long-term attitudinal shifts that are manifested in individuals taking new or different actions that collectively create change
- is achieved when a sufficient number of community members and thought leaders have galvanized around an issue to form a

new or different set of fundamental community expectations

This approach to change recognizes the tremendous power of individual and community values in framing individual and community attitudes and behaviors. It recognizes that it is unreasonable to try to change people's values and focuses instead on identifying and understanding how existing values can serve as links to an issue.

For example, thirty years ago, smoking when and where a person chose was considered a right, closely linked to the normative American value of individual rights. Smokers and the tobacco industry were deeply entrenched. However, emerging research about the dangers of secondhand smoke gave advocates of smoke-free public spaces an opportunity to reframe the argument. Using public will building techniques, advocates demonstrated that exposure to secondhand smoke infringed on others' individual rights to protect their health. Leveraging the closely held value placed on self-determination and individual rights, the priority became personal health over personal choice. Today, smoke-free spaces are the norm.

The Four Principles of Public Will Building

Public will building is grounded in four underlying principles, which together form the foundation for successful development of social change efforts using this model. While each of the principles is independently present in many other forms of social marketing and communication, the synergy and strength of the combined principles make public will building distinctive.

1. *Connecting through closely held values.* Values trump data when it comes to decision making. People make decisions consciously and unconsciously based on their values, and then utilize data to rationalize and support their choice. For individuals to maintain a lasting commitment to an issue as a personal priority, and to hold a conviction that leads to action, the issue must connect to closely held personal values. Individual choices to speak out or take action on an issue flow from resonance between the issue and a person's core value system.

We can and do make isolated decisions based upon specific needs or situations. However, in order to sustain commitment and take actions that may involve risk, an issue must connect with a person's core val-

ues. Public will building acknowledges that trying to change or teach new values is extremely difficult and often threatening. By finding an existing core value and linking an issue to it, a group or individual advocating for social change can create a strong and engaging platform for communication that results in long-term attitudinal and behavioral shifts supported through decisive action.

Establishing the connection with closely held values is best accomplished by designing messages based on those values. As with other forms of persuasive communication, this is achieved through the selection of stories that carry the message, the choice of language used in everything from the name of the effort to the style of writing, and the selection of messengers who share values with the audiences.

2. *Respecting cultural context.* To engage in any meaningful discourse involving closely held values and to create ownership of an issue, understanding and working within a person's or group's cultural context are a necessity. It is important for public will organizers to understand the dynamics of power, language, relationships, values, traditions, worldview, and decision making in a given cultural context. This understanding influences organizers' effective selection of leadership, messengers, messages, strategies, tactics, and tools. Working in accord with the cultural context is an important aspect of any successful communication effort. However, it is essential in public will building because critical aspects of the work rely upon audiences connecting an issue with their core values and upon engaging grassroots and community-based leadership.

3. *Including target audiences in development and testing.* Building public will is dependent upon creating legitimate ownership and engagement in the process by the people affected by an issue in order to result in action and sustained motivation. The public will building process therefore must involve true representation of target audiences in the research, design, development, and testing of key strategies and messages. Inclusion of audiences in all aspects of an effort ensures authenticity, clarity of message, and credibility of messengers. By seeking a deeper level of involvement from their audiences, public will organizers garner perspective and ideas while building a base of grassroots support throughout the planning and implementation process.

4. *Integrating grassroots and traditional communication methods.* Connecting to values is most effectively accomplished through relationships of trust and relies upon direct grassroots outreach where peers, friends,

neighbors, family members, co-workers, and other trusted community members connect members of their circles of influence or social networks to an issue through a motivating value, and actively seek their support and action. Public will building efforts integrate grassroots outreach with advertising and other traditional communication methods to create a fertile environment for outreach and to motivate and reinforce focus on the issue, key messages, and calls to action. This integrated approach is a major distinguishing factor between public will building and more general public awareness building work.

Building Public Will vs. Influencing Public Opinion

Too often, social change communication is focused on short-term wins and symptoms, rather than on tackling the root causes of problems or needs. Such efforts are concentrated on changing public opinion—a short-term gain.

Public opinion-based campaigns are designed to move a target audience to share an opinion linked to a specific issue. Campaigns designed to influence public opinion can be very effective in winning or influencing specific decisions and actions during a specific time frame—such as electing a candidate or passing an initiative. However, this very strength creates vulnerability because public opinion can be effectively swayed and changed back and forth utilizing the same techniques. Communication to sway public opinion tends to identify a winning message for the short term and drive it home through concentrating efforts on the most expedient delivery mechanism, often placing the vast majority of resources into mass media. By its nature, public opinion-based communication seeks to narrow the discourse and discourage personal exploration of and engagement with an issue.

In contrast, public will-based strategies focus on long-term change built over time by engaging broad-based grassroots support to influence individual and institutional change. While public will-based strategies also have clear and measurable goals, they focus on developing a sustainable platform for change and thus invest in greater audience engagement.

Often the need for clear and immediate change (victory at the ballot box, for example) drives the decision to use public opinion-based strategies. This approach often leads to a series of zero-sum wins and losses related to an issue that create specific changes without instilling new community norms or changing baseline expectations about an issue. Further, the messages that are effective in winning a one-time decision can create divisions and/or undermine movement building.

The Five Phases of Public Will Building

Shaping public will on any issue requires a multidimensional approach to changing attitudes and influencing behavior. The five phases of public will building define both the steps that organizers must go through in order to trigger widespread public will building and those that audiences must go through in order to change their internal constructs. The phases of public will building are

Phase 1. Framing and defining the problem or need

Phase 2. Building awareness about the problem or need

Phase 3. Becoming knowledgeable/transmitting information about where and how the problem can be affected or changed

When the Short-Term Message Does Long-Term Harm

Messages used to fight industrial water polluters have "shut off" many of the big industrial offenders, which means that the primary source of water pollution now comes from non-source-point pollution—the individual actions of the general public. However, the same messages that convinced the public that the main cause of water pollution is big industry have resulted in individuals and families discounting the possibility that they personally have any impact on clean water. In addition, the messages have set up an environment vs. economy dichotomy, which has limited common-ground approaches.

Phase 4. Creating a personal conviction (among key audiences) that change needs to occur and issuing a call to action

Phase 5. Evaluating while reinforcing

With any given issue, audience segments are at different levels of interest and engagement, so the phases do not necessarily occur simultaneously for all audiences. Organizers will often interact with audience segments across the spectrum of the public will building phases. For each phase we examine the activities of organizers and the engagement of audiences. We will illustrate each phase with an example. In the techniques section in this chapter's appendix, you will find more information about tactics and tools that help implement a public will building initiative.

PHASE 1:
Framing and Defining the Problem or Need

Individuals and organizations define issues and needs in relationship to the context that they are in and the relationship of each issue and need to their personal values. In the early stages of awareness, audiences self-define issues as having relevance and/or impact. The definition phase creates the context in which an issue or problem is viewed.

ORGANIZERS
In this phase organizers clarify the problem that needs to be addressed by conducting research to develop a clear knowledge base about

- the causes of the problem
- the cultural context
- the entities that have the ability to affect it
- current activities and players involved in seeking and/or blocking change
- gaps in the change effort
- the impacts of the problem (economic, social, political, environmental)

Based upon a clear definition of the problem, the players, and the impacts of the problem, organizers evaluate and identify the best pathway to achieve change. Pathways to change can range from passing new legislation or adjusting administrative rules and procedures to motivating voluntary compliance and market or social pressure that mandate change. The appropriate organizational model and leadership needs for the public will building effort are established based upon the pathway selected.

AUDIENCES

In the first phase of public will building, the pioneering audience is the group that becomes aware and frames an issue as having relevance, and are the early adopters of a public will building initiative. For example, many mainstream audiences' early awareness of clean water needs stemmed from awareness of the relationship between drinking water and health. Their definition, or framing, of the problem is the need for clean drinking water for themselves and their communities.

Key audiences are

- moving from unaware of the problem to early awareness that frames the issue as one of relevance to them

Public will organizers are

- conducting research about the problem
- determining the values with which it connects and the audiences for whom it has the most relevance
- identifying potential change agents and pathways to change
- framing the issue so it has relevance

CASE EXAMPLE: INFORMATION ACCESS ALLIANCE

In the past two decades, median prices for scholarly journals from commercial and nonprofit publishers rose more than 170 percent—a rate significantly higher than the rate of inflation. This is a particular problem in scientific, technical, and medical (STM) journals and legal serials publishing. Pricing, as well as practices like bundling for electronic publications, makes it increasingly difficult for libraries to acquire materials to meet their customers' needs. This results in decreased access to these valued publications.

Building on work done by groups such as the Scholarly Publishing and Academic Resources Coalition (SPARC), an arm of the Association of Research Libraries (ARL), a coalition of organizations, including SPARC and ARL, the American Library Association, Association of College and Research Libraries, American Association of Law Libraries, Medical Library Association, and Special Libraries Association formed the Information Access Alliance (IAA) in 2003 to address this challenge and advocate for change in the way state and federal antitrust enforcement agencies examine merger transactions in the serials publishing industry.

IAA identified the harmful effects of reduced access to serial publications and placed the issue in the context of the societal benefits that result from having broad access. Members of the coalition—including library staff, economists, and policy analysts—explored the reduced opportunity to build off the learning of others; the decreased innovation in STM fields; and the long-term economic impact. Through this analysis, coalition members identified the benefits reaped both by members of these specialized fields and the general public and established a framework that positions access to scholarly work as critical to the health and wealth of society.

By detaining the value of these publications in this context, IAA effectively framed the issue of decreased access as a threat to core social values, including health, innovation, and prosperity. This framing was used by IAA in direct communication with the U.S. Department of Justice, key congressional representatives, scholars, and community leaders through white papers, direct outreach, and a broad symposium cosponsored by IAA and the American Antitrust Institute on the effects of publisher mergers. Speakers at the symposium—including librarians, economists, and lawyers—focused on the economics of libraries

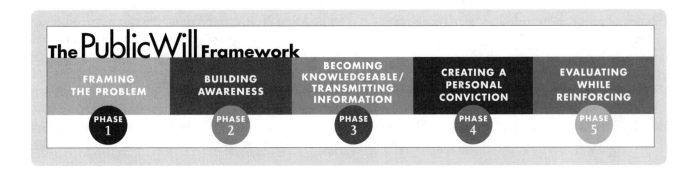

and the publishing industry, the history and outcomes of mergers, and possible remedies.

IAA's demonstration of what is at risk created a strong motivator for broad involvement by all participants and community opinion leaders in advocacy efforts to encourage the Department of Justice to change the criteria it uses to evaluate publisher mergers.

PHASE 2:
Building Awareness about the Problem or Need

ORGANIZERS

Organizers are building awareness about the problem or need through outreach aimed at educating, raising awareness, and building interest about the issue by connecting it with existing core value(s) of priority audiences.

To build awareness, organizers identify the audience segments that can affect the issue and gather information about each segment's level of awareness, relationship to the issue, personal values, and sources of information. This information helps organizers prioritize the audiences, develop effective messages, and select the best channels to deliver the messages and build awareness. Messages are tested with audiences for resonance and impact, and are customized with audience involvement to work within the cultural context of each audience segment.

Information is conveyed through integrated grassroots outreach and traditional media techniques. Grassroots outreach provides direct person-to-person communication to connect the issue to existing values, deliver messages with veracity and validity, and create engagement and ownership.

Traditional communication tools such as media relations and advertising, along with brochures, pamphlets, web content, events and activities, etc., reinforce direct outreach by supporting early adopters in their commitment to champion the issue, creating a fertile environment in which others become willing and ready to discuss the issue, and providing environmental cues that provide a sense of being part of a larger movement.

AUDIENCES

Once an issue or problem is defined, audience awareness and knowledge must increase in order to raise the importance and relevance of the issue. By gaining deeper awareness of the issue, including examples of impacts, underlying causes, supporters, and opponents, and how it relates to core values, audiences become ready to "own" the issue. Also in this phase, audiences are participating in research conducted by public will organizers. (Participating in this research is one mechanism through which their awareness is raised.)

Key audiences are

- participating in testing of messages, campaign collateral, etc.
- gaining awareness and depth of information through trusted relationships, affiliations, media, etc.

Public will organizers are

- preparing: segmenting, learning about and prioritizing audiences, crafting messages, identifying communication channels
- attracting early adopters and key influencers
- building awareness through grassroots and traditional media

CASE EXAMPLE: "LEE Y SERÁS"

Scholastic, the National Council of La Raza (NCLR), and Verizon came together to develop "Lee y serás" (read and you will become), a national, multiyear initiative that supports parents and communities in building early literacy skills among Latino children from birth to age eight. Having identified a problem, the organizers moved to the second phase, building awareness. Currently, 86 percent of Latino fourth-graders and 91 percent of eighth-graders read at or below basic skill levels, and less than 25 percent of Latino seventeen-year-olds can read at the skill level necessary for success in college. This literacy gap actually begins before children enter kindergarten. The goal of "Lee y serás" is to create long-term attitudinal and behavior changes that close the gap for Latino children. Organizers engaged academic researchers, key community institutions, business people, literacy organizations, and affiliates of NCLR in program development, building a base of early adopters and key influencers who could both help the organizers learn as much as possible about the issue as well as serve as trusted sources of information with their own constituencies to establish the need for action.

Organizers also brought together Latino families and learned that while the Latino culture has a rich storytelling tradition, many non-English-speaking parents were fearful that storytelling or reading to children in Spanish might harm the child's ability to succeed in learning to read or speak English at school. In addition, many of these parents viewed education as something that begins in school instead of seeing themselves as the children's first and most important teachers and role models. This input shaped a grass-roots outreach campaign that connects back with individual families through community organizations, social networks, and libraries to give parents what they need to help their children succeed in school and in life.

PHASE 3:
Becoming Knowledgeable/Transmitting Information about Where and How the Problem Can Be Affected or Changed

ORGANIZERS
During the third phase, outreach moves from focusing on raising awareness of the problem to providing information about how change can occur and what needs to be done to trigger change. Since audiences are aware of the issue and are seeking ways to have an impact, organizers now focus on providing specific information about how to affect change through personal actions (environmental, parenting, health, and other behaviors) and through community and institutional actions (voting, voicing support or opposition to a policy, purchasing behaviors/voting with one's dollars, adopting new policies, practices or procedures, etc.).

AUDIENCES
Once audiences are aware of an issue and are gaining knowledge of its importance, relevance, and impact, they want to know how to make a difference. They seek answers to questions including the following:

- Who can affect the issue?
- What organizations are responsible and able to make a difference?
- What can I do about it?

As they find the answers to these questions, audiences begin to connect their related values and awareness of the issue with knowledge of what they can do about it.

Key audiences are

- hearing about the issue through multiple channels with identification of specific desired changes and the mechanisms for change

Public will organizers are

- transmitting information with specifics on desired changes and the mechanisms for change

CASE EXAMPLE: KING COUNTY LIBRARY SYSTEM
Washington State's King County Library System (KCLS) successfully raised awareness among key audiences in 2004 when it sought to educate customers about the capital needs for the growing regional library system. KCLS needed to make sure that people understood both the upcoming expiration of the capital bond and how the replacement bond would fund the facilities, maintenance, and improvements that library users said they strongly valued. A community survey was conducted to gauge those aspects of the system that were most important to the community and a series of listening sessions was conducted through the service area to hear directly from customers what they most wanted and valued.

KCLS then created a message framework that reflected back to the community what the library had learned about the community's desire for quality facilities and technology, lifelong learning opportunities and educational support, and expanded or new facilities. The bond education effort created opportunities for sharing information at meetings of community organizations, through material provided on the website and direct mail, and through specific, detailed information in each branch about improvements and changes that would result from the funding. Through these efforts the library was able to convey effectively its commitment to delivering on community needs and expectations.

A separate, privately funded bond advocacy campaign by community members then built upon the baseline of community knowledge to promote the specific action needed to ensure capital funding for the library system: passage of the bond. The bond advocacy campaign asked the community to take action in support of the library system by voting yes on the ballot measure that authorized the capital bond. The community did so with more than 63 percent of the vote.

PHASE 4:
Creating a Personal Conviction (among Key Audiences) That Change Needs to Occur and Issuing a Call to Action

ORGANIZERS

In order to help individuals make a personal commitment, public will building organizers are delivering clear call-to-action messages that encourage both making a lasting commitment and taking specific actions that affect the issue.

Using the integrated grassroots and traditional media approach, the call to action should be delivered by champions and ambassadors (see the appendix) as direct requests and supported through messages in the media and communication materials. The call to action should be framed with an awareness of the overall context so that individual commitments and changes are positioned as part of new and aspirational community expectations. The call to action should primarily drive a particular choice and behavior that create greater commitment to the issue. In addition to more traditional calls to action that include advocacy, purchasing, and voting decisions, organizers may encourage audiences to make pledges, endorse core positions, and identify themselves as part of a movement.

AUDIENCES

In this phase, audiences have a strong awareness of the issue, understand how it connects to their values, and see how they can influence it. Now audience members are moved to make a personal commitment that change needs to occur and that they need to be part of it.

This is the critical stage where individuals make a choice (conscious or unconscious) either to own and affect an issue or to merely be aware of it. This commitment to creating change goes beyond a choice in a specific election or being for or against a particular piece of legislation. Commitment in this phase means that people understand the problem—and its root causes—and dedicate themselves to working for change through a variety of actions. It is in this phase that the issue becomes a touch point in individual choice, influencing how people vote, what they purchase, and to what positions they lend or deny their support. It is at this point that public will is established.

Key audiences are

- gaining a sense of ownership/dedication to affecting the problem and its causes

- identifying specific actions to take
- committing themselves to making a difference
- taking action and recruiting others to take action

Public will organizers are

- providing tangible opportunities for committed audiences to take action

CASE EXAMPLE: MULTNOMAH COUNTY LIBRARY

Let's return to Multnomah County Library. This library system has effectively built public will over nearly fifteen years. Looking at what it has done through the public will building lens, we see that the library first framed its issue as "the library is a critical educational and cultural resource." Then it raised awareness that a great library is key to a great community. It transmitted information that change was needed to ensure a great library. And in Phase Four, it instilled in the community the notion that action was required, in the form of significant investment in the capital infrastructure.

As a result, a significant percentage of voters acted on their personal conviction that their community needed to financially support a great library. This shift in public will ensured the passage of a bond measure in the early 1990s to renovate the Central Library and to build new facilities or renovate all of the branches. It also resulted in $4.5 million in private capital, including $1 million raised in approximately ninety days through a mass appeal campaign. This was the first significant private philanthropy in the community in decades, and philanthropic support continues to grow to this day. In 1997, voters subsequently passed an expanded operating levy that extended hours and increased collections.

PHASE 5:
Evaluating while Reinforcing

ORGANIZERS

Public will building organizers must evaluate the approach being used and its impact while continually reinforcing those who have made the choice to take action. By evaluating messages, activities, and results, and linking successes and failures to specific strategies, organizers can make adjustments to strategy and modify the approach to achieve greater impact.

Evaluation allows for the development of new tools and strategies to make supporters more effective.

Unlike many public opinion-based efforts where the key focus is on undecided audiences, public will organizers focus significant attention on ensuring that both grassroots and traditional media communication reinforce audiences that have made the choice to act. This reinforcement component is critical to public will building because it helps ensure that once people have moved an issue into their sphere of priorities, they are reminded of their commitment and continue to see it as part of how they and their community define themselves.

AUDIENCES

Once individuals have taken action, they evaluate the results of their action, become increasingly aware of the positions and actions of others in relationship to the issue, and either reinforce their decision and deepen their conviction or question their decision and make adjustments to their actions. The more they feel reinforced in their choice, the more they will take actions consistent with their conviction to help drive change and influence others.

Key audiences are

- being exposed to messages/actions that validate their choices and encourage continued action and the recruitment of others

Public will organizers are

- evaluating effectiveness of tools and messages
- adapting as necessary
- supporting/reinforcing audiences that have taken action

CASE EXAMPLE: WASHINGTON STATE LIBRARY

In 2004, Washington State Library (WSL) secured funding to conduct a multiyear, statewide marketing effort for libraries of all types. A library marketing committee was established to represent the needs and interests of a diverse array of libraries and demographics throughout the state. WSL launched a broad-based campaign that included a media component, materials development and distribution, and extensive training for libraries on effective marketing strategies. The organization conducted special outreach to school and academic libraries to address their unique needs. Presentations—to leadership groups, trustees, and at conferences—were used to ensure the broadest reach, flexibility, and support for everyone choosing to participate.

Significant data collected in the first year were used to adapt the campaign for subsequent years. This evaluation process identified a need to tweak the campaign communication tools to include the audiences libraries serve more directly. For example, the newer materials allowed placement of text and branding elements by individual library systems. Also, in year one the campaign told the story of customers, but in year two the campaign shifted to a first-person, active, and authentic voice where the customers told stories themselves. To reinforce the commitment of early adopters, WSL extended advanced training and support for individual marketing efforts to libraries that had taken action.

Conclusion

Public will building is a powerful approach to creating sustainable change that ensures libraries are viewed as critical to vibrant, healthy communities. The process attracts and enlists committed champions and ambassadors who are moved to conviction, whose conviction becomes action, and whose action garners the conviction and action of others. As change occurs, evaluation and reinforcement support the efforts of early adopters, converting them to ambassadors. Ultimately, this establishes a new set of normative community expectations within which our communities—and our libraries—can thrive.

The public will building approach achieves high advancement of mission with high return on investment by leveraging the efforts and resources of supporters, by selecting strategies that have long-term impact, and by linking issues with existing values to create long-term commitment. It creates a sustainable platform for change and moves an issue forward to become a touch point for an individual's voting, purchasing, or other decision making. The techniques that follow in the appendix provide tips and tactical options for public will building and other sustainable change efforts.

Advocating and creating change through the public will building process establishes the values-based commitment and the rationale for support of libraries as part of the expectations of a community. This makes it more likely that changes will last and that additional and perhaps more difficult challenges will be surmounted in the future. Due to its capacity- and movement-building nature, the public will building process also grows leaders and networks that have greater voice and power with which to affect other issues and unleash the potential of their communities.

APPENDIX
Techniques for Building Public Will

The public will building model integrates a complex set of theories from communication, social marketing, community organizing, and engagement. However, the greater depth and breadth of public will building requires several fundamentals that warrant particular attention due to their unique application in the process. The sections below focus on these key techniques and indicate the phases in which they occur.

1. Pathways to Change—
Public Will Building Phase 1

Selecting the best pathway to achieving the desired change relies on

- an analysis of where audiences are in the stages of change
- the power within the culture of the values to which the issue will be connected
- the approach that best balances achievable and demonstrable results with true impact significant enough to ignite normative expectations and aspiration

Identification of the allies and opponents of the desired change, their reasons, and the strength of their positions on the issue, as well as the ability of sponsors to leverage and drive the change process, and the cultural context in which the change is sought all need to be considered in selection of the best pathway. Pathway options include the following:

Seek voluntary change as a precursor or alternative to mandated change. This pathway applies where administrative decision making is used to demonstrate the efficacy of alternative approaches and policies or where business and/or labor elects to make changes. Examples: Fast-tracking and streamlining of permitting and licensing procedures by public sector administrators and conservation of water and energy by consumers are examples of voluntary actions that can test or pilot the potential for mandated change.

Relate change to the value for which there is the greatest agreement. This pathway applies where the initial change has significant common ground and is used as a first step to establish trust and results. Example: The

establishment of smoke-free workplaces was one of the first major changes in the United States' "tobacco wars." Workplaces went smoke-free long before public spaces, because of common ground agreement that individuals without freedom of movement (workers who are assigned to a workspace) deserve the right to make their own choices about their health, including not wanting to inhale smoke.

Build a new status quo and then legislate long-term change. This pathway applies where key influencers can create enough grassroots voluntary action and market/social pressure on the issue that the normative way of operating is changed and legislation is used to codify it. Examples: Voluntary carbon reduction actions, sourcing of recycled paper, supply chain auditing, and the use of certified forest products are all examples of pioneering behavior moving to the mainstream and legislation following the new realities in the marketplace.

Seek mandatory change (policy, education, and enforcement). This pathway applies where the need to remove barriers and to establish change that will create consequences and costs for vested interests requires policy mandates with enforcement authority through the legislative or judicial process. Examples: Environmental regulation of industrial polluters, changes in capital requirements for new businesses, and elimination of duplicative tax structures all require policy change.

2. Movement Building—
Public Will Building Phase 1

The goal of public will building is to create long-term change and requires selection of the right leadership and organizational model to best guide the desired change in a given environment.

LEADERSHIP TYPES
Based upon the change desired and the factors outlined in the "Pathways to Change" section, organizers need to clarify the types of leader(s) needed for success. Different efforts may need different leadership types at different times as they evolve. This may be accomplished by having different leaders or by the same individuals evolving their style of leadership to fit the

changing needs of a project. Several types of leaders have been defined by numerous management theorists, including these:

The visionary—helps others recognize a new idea or possibility. This is often the type of leader needed when key challenges to success include lack of recognition that there is a problem, hopelessness that change can occur, or lack of ability to envision aspirational change due to oppression or a sense of being powerless. In these instances, it is critical that the cause has a leader who can not only garner attention for the issue, but can also inspire others to envision a better reality and believe that change is possible. Initiators at the beginning of a process most commonly play this role. Visionaries can evolve to playing the role of agitator, though often the visionary transitions the leadership role to an agitator who advances the cause more aggressively.

The agitator—demands that the issue gets on the table, channels the frustration and readiness for change that already exist in others, and illustrates the costs of not embracing change. The agitator often demands extreme change from which compromise (beyond what many had thought possible) is negotiated. This role is played during the phase when the most aggressive change efforts are being championed. It is rare that the person in this role can transition into the next leadership role required, the diplomat.

The diplomat—brings all parties to the table, is able to find the common ground, identifies areas for compromise, engages the power structure in being part of the process, and develops shared ownership of the issue and required change. The diplomat is often seen as a sustainer of change and as an incremental change advocate. Diplomats often are responsible for extending the reach of a given social change agenda to new audiences. It is possible for the diplomat to transition to the role of manager, but frequently the diplomat becomes bored with that role and will seek new avenues for bridge building outside the movement.

The manager—leverages the skills, connections, and resources of others dedicated to change; creates systems that reinforce the commitments that have been made; ensures that the impacts of change are reinvested in sustaining work on the issue; and serves as the long-range strategist who moves the normative community expectations in a succession of logical changes. The manager is a sustainer. While often the profile of the movement is lower during the manager's tenure, this role is vital to the long-term nature of public will building efforts. Often when a manager leaves the role, others engaged may find themselves seeking visionary or agitator personalities to reinvigorate the change movement.

Early awareness of leadership needs can help public will organizers identify and recruit the right mix of people to work on the effort and fill in the gaps. It is important to be aware of the need for different leadership attributes at different stages of building public will and to be willing and able to transition the style of the leader(s).

Often, there is a need for various styles of leadership at the same time. For example, the agitator and diplomat can make a very effective team to push the envelope on an issue while garnering actual change. It is not unusual to find that the founders of a movement possess passion and vision, but do not possess the full spectrum of leadership styles needed. Effective advocates will recognize this in themselves and bring in the styles that are needed to achieve success.

ORGANIZATIONAL STRUCTURE

Determining and developing the appropriate organizational structure to facilitate progress should be based upon the same criteria as the selection of leadership. Questions to consider include

- How long does the effort need to be sustained?
- Do we need participants to represent constituencies or to serve as members of a brain trust?
- What is the level of commitment we can ask for and garner?
- Based upon whom we aim to influence, what structure will be the most powerful and have the most leverage?

Some of the typical options for organizational structure include

Network—an affiliation of individuals and organizations that join around a common interest in which each member makes commitments and participates on a case-by-case basis.

Coalition—a collection of organizations committed to a common issue or cause, often for a defined period of time or through the achievement of specific change(s). Each member organization has made clear commitments to participate and generally represents the point of view and needs of a constituency. Members carry the responsibility of communicating to and activating their constituency.

Alliance—a long-term coalition dedicated to an issue that will encompass many individual efforts and which is central to the mission of all members.

Initiative—a time-specific or limited-scope project for which individuals and organizations make a one-time commitment.

Stand-alone entity—an organization dedicated to working on an issue for the long term, often supported by and working to coordinate the efforts of other organization participants in initiatives, networks, and coalitions.

3. Audience Identification, Segmentation, and Prioritization— Public Will Building Phase 2

Within each audience group there is a spectrum of attitudes and levels of interest and awareness about a given issue. Understanding this spectrum helps identify those most receptive to the message; those most likely to take action and make behavioral change; and those most likely to encourage change in others. The same analysis also identifies audience segments that are unlikely to change. Achieving lasting social change depends on first reaching audience members who will be early adopters and whose involvement will have the greatest impact on moving others to take action.

To understand how best to connect with audience segments and identify where they are in the public will building phases, audience research focuses on identifying each segment's

- needs
- values that connect with the issue
- key levers for action, points of resistance
- competing values
- trusted messengers and conduits of information
- levels of commitment to creating specific change(s)

Using this analysis, public will organizers segment an audience based upon each segment's relationship to the issue, readiness for action, and potential to affect the selected pathway to change. Once segmentation is accomplished, each audience is prioritized with respect to goals and time line for the effort. Generally, efforts in public will building campaigns are focused on providing a fertile environment and easy-to-use communication tools so that audience members in the later phases of public will building (conviction/action and reinforcement) can reach and influence audiences in the earlier phases. Both the mass media and grassroots aspects of the approach reach and move audience members in the building awareness phase.

4. Influence Mapping— Public Will Building Phase 2

Influence mapping is a technique that helps focus outreach and grassroots implementation. It can be completed both at the macro level (determining which individuals and organizations have significant influence with each major audience segment) and at an individual level (determining the sphere of influence for each key champion we have identified). This technique is useful to identify the most powerful links to activate individuals, institutions, and communities.

To map spheres of influence, organizers first look at each priority audience segment and identify voices that have credibility with and the respect and trust of the audience—we call this validity of voice. Those with validity of voice can include respected individuals, formal and informal leaders (particularly important based upon the cultural context), media and other preferred communication channels, trusted advisors, and members of business, civic, faith, and advocacy organizations. Based upon this initial charting, people can then be categorized as potential champions or ambassadors.

Champions are individuals or organizations that are recognized formal or informal leaders with significant influence, mechanisms, and capacity for outreach. They have the ability to recruit and encourage participation of significant audience segments.

Ambassadors are individuals or organizations that commit to exerting influence in their work and/or personal and civic lives. They generally are early adopters of an issue who will encourage participation and engagement of others in their close circle.

After charting influence maps for each segment, it is good to repeat the exercise to look individually at each champion and ambassador and to map each person's specific sphere of influence on audience segments, organizations, communities, and other individual champions. Public will organizers can base the prioritization and order of outreach on the individuals and organizations that have the greatest potential to be champions and/or have the reach and trust as ambassadors to influence a critical early audience.

5. Integrating Grassroots and Traditional Media—Public Will Building Phases 2 and 3

Public will building integrates high-profile media and partnership strategies with grassroots social movement techniques. Traditional social marketing/public opinion campaigns often put the lion's share of planning and resources into the media components, with the grassroots treated as fill-in or a low budget priority.

When the goal is to connect an issue with existing closely held values, grassroots outreach (person-to-person contact) is imperative. For audiences to interact with and relate to a message at a deep personal level, establishing trust, engagement, discourse and "connection" are imperative. Ensuring that individuals and groups in the *conviction* and *reinforcement* phases are empowered and enabled to carry the messages to others leverages the most valuable asset of a cause: existing trusted relationships. Personal outreach that directly engages peers and invites them to join with the person making the *ask* turns "passive shareholders" of an issue into "activist investors" for change.

Integrated grassroots action, media, and traditional communication tools (brochures, posters, handbills, websites, blogs, etc.) are utilized to achieve two goals; The first goal is to create a fertile environment for grassroots connections by creating awareness of the issue and establishing that there is significant interest and momentum behind it. The second is to motivate and reinforce individuals who have made the commitment to take action. Media presence provides champions and ambassadors with direct motivation and encouragement and builds their confidence by conveying that they are part of something that has currency and importance in their community.

To be effective in this integrated approach, all communication tools need to be developed and tested with the involvement and feedback of grassroots champions and ambassadors to ensure validity and reliability. Furthermore, tools and messages must be provided to grassroots partners in formats that allow easy incorporation into their communication (e.g., camera-ready artwork for newsletters, easily co-branded content for websites, talking points with current stories, and examples of relevance). Moreover, the timing and placement of media should support outreach efforts by grassroots champions, including key events such as legislative days; advocacy pushes, conferences, and summits; key cycles in government decision making; high-profile international visits and events, etc. Finally, media outreach serves to encourage individuals and organizations that are not yet on the radar of the campaign to identify themselves and engage with the effort as new ambassadors and champions.

6. Creating Personal Conviction— Public Will Building Phase 4

In the fourth phase of public will building, audience members make a personal commitment that moves the issue into their own set of priority causes. Once this occurs, the issue truly becomes a touch point for long-term decision making that influences individual behaviors such as voting, purchasing, and advocacy. Creating a personal conviction is very different than committing to take a specific action on a specific day.

While public will organizers will want and need individuals and organizations to take specific actions, it is cementing a personal conviction to the issue as represented through one's core values that creates resiliency and ongoing commitment that affects multiple choices in the long term. Integrating grassroots and traditional media communication helps build conviction and is supported and augmented by the use of overt tools for commitment. The tools will vary based upon the issue being addressed and the cultural context of the community. A couple of examples follow.

Pledges are written commitments to championing a cause with both general statements of support and specific actions. This tool is most powerful when it is both retained by the person or organization that makes the pledge (to serve as a reminder and as a plan of action) and is also shared with others either through a peer swap approach or through centralized collection of commitments. Peer swaps are a method of creating reinforcement and accountability on projects where the organizational capacity for staff follow-up does not exist. In this approach, each individual or organization that makes a pledge keeps a copy and exchanges a copy with a peer. Each party agrees to check in with the peer at set intervals (three months, six months, a year) to provide support, encouragement, and reminders. To create momentum and identify results, it is often helpful to seek permission to publish a list of those who make pledges. In a centralized collection model, the public will sponsor or a partner organization receives all of the pledges and ensures that follow-up occurs at set intervals by volunteers or staff.

Declarations are the signing of a statement of commitment or formally endorsing a cause or an initiative. Declarations are generally less specific than pledges and serve to establish a growing base of support, create agreement on general principles, and drive accountability for leaders, policy-makers, and organizations. To leverage impact of the declaration, signers and endorsers should receive a copy. Where culturally appropriate, these copies should be in a format that encourages posting or other forms of distribution and acknowledgment. Organizers should request permission, then publish and update the list of signers to create momentum and increase credibility.

7. Continual Evaluation and Evolution—Public Will Building Phase 5

Ensuring that resources are deployed as effectively as possible and that results are being achieved require public will organizers to include ongoing evaluation and evolution. At each stage in the process, understanding how success will be measured, analyzing the impacts of each strategy, listening to and observing grassroots partners' use and modification of tools, and making appropriate adjustments will increase the public will campaign's impact. At the beginning of the process, public will organizers should identify key measures of success and establish clear baseline measures. Measurements can include

Activities—pledges and endorsements, introduction of reform proposals, establishment of organizations and networks, etc.

Outcomes—policy change, number of affordable housing units, percentage of low birthweight babies, measures of water or air quality, home ownership rates, job growth, per capita income changes, carbon sequestration, etc.

Comparative indicators—comparative statistics on outcomes with peer communities, attitudinal indicators (measurable changes in attitudes and opinions)

Beyond measuring results and impacts, it is important to establish a protocol for continual evolution of strategy, messages, organizational structure, and leadership. Results should be tracked as audience segments move through phases of public will building.

It is of particular importance to look at how grassroots partners adapt or modify strategies, messages, and tools. In many social marketing efforts, organizers only track adoption of tactics by the grassroots (who and how many have signed up to participate) and do not track how the grassroots innovates and modifies tools. By engaging grassroots participants in the evaluation and feedback process and by observing how strategies change when put to use in the field, public will organizers can hone their strategies and messages to be more effective. This approach also allows for easier recruitment of ambassadors and champions through use of language and tools that better resonate in the community. Finally, the evaluation/evolution protocol serves to reinforce the commitment of existing champions who experience true ownership by seeing their ideas adopted.

8. Sustainability through Reinforcement—All Phases of Public Will Building

Public will-based change must be resilient to establish, maintain, and grow new sets of normative community expectations. To a great degree, this is accomplished through the very approach taken to create the change. As outlined above, this approach includes clear identification and framing of an issue in relationship to existing values, real engagement, and ownership of key actors; momentum building through integrated media and grassroots outreach; and evolution of strategies in real time to improve impact and address new challenges and opportunities.

The sustainability of this work is significantly increased through overt recognition that the effort does not end with the call to action or the commitment of audiences to take action. In public will building, specific strategies are established to reinforce the choices and commitments made by ambassadors and champions. The reinforcement also provides confirmation to these advocates that their work is making a difference and creating real change. Public will organizers accomplish reinforcement by putting in place communication mechanisms to acknowledge, thank, and update individuals and organizations that have made a commitment and taken action. These mechanisms include direct outreach and updates in the format that is most comfortable for the audience (including letters, e-mail, web-based updates, personal meetings, phone calls, text messages, etc.) and through the message design of media and communication tools. Use of community building tactics such as celebrations, demonstrations, networks, online communities, summits, conferences, events, and peer swap relationships help empower champions and ambassadors to provide confirmation to each other.

Note

The authors would like to acknowledge Metropolitan Group's clients, from whom they've learned so much; the libraries and library associations who have shared their stories for this chapter; and Jeannette Pai-Espinosa and Jennifer Gilstrap Hearn, who contributed to the development of Metropolitan Group's public will building framework.

3

CAN ALL THIS 2.0 STUFF HELP LIBRARIES WITH PROMOTION AND COMMUNICATE OUR VALUE?

Stephen Abram

I recall times in my early career when I spoke at a lot of sessions about library marketing and public relations. It was the early 1980s and the beginning of the age of electronic librarianship. We were promoting our newly developed skills in online searching (Ha! at 300 baud!) and our new positioning in electronic research. It was the early days of the discussion with words like *cybraries, paperless, virtual,* and *digital.* We were thrilled that online research seemed to be a guarantee of job security—just like those folks over in the word processing centers! Ah, nostalgia doesn't protect. The changes have run unabated from the commercial Internet to the Web to 2.0 and virtual worlds like Second Life. And we're still challenged to communicate our role for better understanding of our value.

Why? I suspect that we're not being assertive enough. Too many of us try to influence subtly. Too many of us are not direct enough. Too many of us only use a small range of the tools in the marketer's toolkit. Many think people will notice the good work we do naturally. (They won't.) And too many of us believe that it's good enough to be right and good, and to tell folks stuff. (It's not.)

What are the basic marketing building blocks? They're simple, really, and classic: place, product, price, promotion, public relations and personal selling. That's the classic marketing mix. We have a great product. Our price is right on. We're everywhere—indeed, in more places than Starbucks or McDonald's. We promote libraries using everything from websites to bookmarks. However, we fall down on the personal selling skills and strategies. Perhaps we feel that since most libraries are free to the end user, we don't need to sell. We fail to understand the nature of influence, social recommendations, and how the politics of our environment works. People pay; they may not always be paying cash directly to us but they are paying in taxes, tuition, time, their career or family success, or in their own personal success. Indeed, *time* often comes out on top in surveys of today's market as the most important factor. How did Ranganathan put it? "Save the time of the reader." Can we promote savings if gas rises to $5 per gallon? Can we save time with e-books and web stations?

Libraries have a lot to promote and sell. Besides our myriad programs and services, we need to influence a lot of other things in our community—like fund-raising goals, budgets and bonds, local awareness of our role in the economy, education, and community success. Can we use our library communications to generate behavioral change? Better educated citizens, higher performing students, better small business success, large industry, and tourism? Can we set our goals high? Can we measure and prove success?

Selling is not a dirty word. Selling is about people, not products, and I believe that libraries are more about people than books. Selling must be baked into the DNA of libraries. Selling is situational. Sustainable selling is about *attitude* more than *aptitude*. You aren't born with the skills, you learn them; selling is a learned professional skill—there's no such thing as a natural. The key is to choose, in every situation, to make a call to action and to ask for the sale—the library transaction, the sign-up, the endorsement, the donation. Are all of our staff and colleagues ready for this step?

I am fascinated by the influencing process and find it very interesting to think about the shift that has happened in influencing tools—driven largely by the new range of Web 2.0 tools that has created a major opportunity to communicate with the citizenry and involve,

motivate, and engage them. I am amazed at how these tools have been used in recent elections in the United States and Canada and how they are materially changing the political process. Can libraries learn from these changes?

So, in an effort to keep you up to date on the key electronic tools being used by folks everywhere, I thought I'd list the main tools that you'll need to be aware of and add to your toolkits for making an even greater difference in your communities. (I am assuming you're already fully cognizant and using the traditional tools like brochures, websites, ads, direct mail, fliers, billboards, banners, and lawn signs.)

Here's a modest list of 2.0 tools I consider pretty important. I haven't included URLs since they're so easy for you to find and I've blogged about many of these at *Stephen's Lighthouse* (http://stephenslight house.sirsidynix.com). Most of these you've seen have a major impact on the last U.S. presidential election and have figured prominently in many other jurisdictions. There are loads of great examples of most in libraries. As always, the best compliment to finding a great idea in another library is to steal it!

1. YouTube

- Every political candidate in Canada and the United States in recent years has had some form of YouTube video. Sometimes they're planned and produced and sometimes they just happen, driven by the competition or the amateur audience and citizen journalists.
- Review the most recent InfoTubey Award winners where you can see many examples of fun and educational library videos.
- Create one—have fun. Viral it; use viral marketing and let it fly. Check to see if any videos about your library have already been posted.
- Try it to demonstrate story hours, teen contests, rock concerts, gaming nights, literacy training, and more—to attract folks to the big events.

2. Second Life

- IBM has 400 employees working on environments for this site! Companies, libraries, and charities are having early successes here. Check out the libraries in Second Life including Alliance Library System, Public Library of Charlotte and Mecklenburg

County, and McMaster University. Also check out American Cancer Society and March of Dimes presences.
- I am told that every U.S. presidential candidate had a presence here.
- Think about this for orientations, events, education, walk-in books, author events, teen outreach, etc.

3. Facebook

- This is the sweet spot for some politicos since it attracts the majority of first- and second-time national voters. My son's Facebook site got him interviewed by the Canadian Press newswire.
- Get a Facebook page for your library, and invite your contacts. Identify personalities of your library and promote them with their own sites. Do you have a budding Nancy Pearl? It's time for librarians to de-cloak; professionals don't hide their identities like Clark Kent.
- Check out the developer resources on the F8 for Facebook Developers (www.facebook .com/f8/) and add your online public access

catalog (OPAC), databases, website links. Try using Facebook for reference queries.

- Understand the power of Facebook groups, political party links, friends' networks, and event features. Can you bring people into your events and programs?

4. MySpace

- This is the granddaddy of big social networks. It's more entertainment and socially oriented, but the average age is reported to be thirty-two—and that's significant.
- Get on MySpace to learn more and look at its use for special markets. Advertisers are big there—politics follows closely.
- Build a personality online—individual staff as well as your institution. Add your OPAC and services. Do invites for events such as Rock the Shelves, Final 4 gaming tournaments, and author readings.
- Connect to local MySpace groups—even local bands and content creators.

5. Flickr

- Collect your pictures in one place and share them with your teams; it's a natural concept for engaging your communities.
- Are you ready to develop tagging rules for library use? Can you approve pictures for wide use?
- Can you collect your volunteers' pictures so that you'll recognize them? Can you get a major collection of library images in one place to foster visual promotion skills?
- Think about genealogy, local history, teens, and seniors. Can you take pictures of your local sites of interest or gravestones and build links to your tourism sector?
- Try holding scanning parties to collect local collections of antique photos.

6. Podcasts

- Check out ODEO or the myriad of other podcasting tools and remember that iTunes is both a platform and distributor.
- Add your voice to the community. Telling stories is at the heart of the influencing process to make your arguments passionately and tell your stories with color.
- Discover your library's voice "personalities" and create library-positive tales. Book

reviews, book chats, and video or game reviews are all positive steps.

- Get your director to podcast—for five minutes, max. Are there other voices that reflect your community—users, staff, trustees?
- Can you find other local podcasts and search the spoken word? Are they in your collection and OPAC?

7. Wikipedia

- Remember that you can create your own wiki with PB Wiki and Media Wiki.
- Check out the Wikipedia entries that matter to your situation—or create one. Have your looked at your institution or city on Wikipedia (www.wikipedia.org)? Check out the competition too. Check out the issues: are the entries balanced?
- Can you set up RSS feeds on the Wikipedia entries that matter to you? Beware of wiki vandalism.

8. Ning

- Create communities within communities. Organize your teams and provide them with access to your community's videos, podcasts, blog postings, links, etc. Ning is a very powerful tool!
- Build a team—private or public—to share information in the context of a bond or budget campaign.
- Can you find and organize your supporters this well? Is this an easy way to start an e-mail or letter-writing campaign?

9. Twitter

- Too poor to afford walkie-talkies at a library event? Try Twitter (or Jaiku) on your mobile phone or laptop and you can keep everyone in contact and informed. Get ready for the trend in microblogging!

10. Mozes

- Looking to build a smart mob? Try building a texting system to local mobile phones (e.g., local press, teams, and library supporters) so that you're connected.
- Can you build a messaging dashboard tied to mailing lists for communicating news, events, ideas, and positions?

11. NowPublic

- Check out more about the revolution in participatory news gathering.
- Try playing with the new Truemors site.
- Push your own news or information.
- Connect with local readers. Can this be a book club?

12. Blogging and RSS

- Yes, blogging seems a no-brainer in the promotion of libraries. Doesn't every library have a half dozen blogs now? But vanilla blogging isn't enough; you need to make sure it's populated—probably by more than one voice. Ensure the words and tags are good for later discovery. Does the local press subscribe to your blog?
- Are you renovating or building a new library? It's a real no-brainer to take a photo every day and engage your community in the project through your blog. Excitement builds—for staff too!
- Are you ready for picture blogs, video blogs, link blogs, and more? All at once?
- Connect your blog to a city or institutional agenda (e.g., the chamber of commerce or board of trade) for extra points.

13. SEO: Search Engine Optimization

- Learn how to do this or hire someone to. It's essential.
- Keep it up to date and make sure that your points of view end up in the major web conversations.
- Search your blog's key words and issues on all search engines (including maps) and make sure your pages are discoverable in the most popular search engines.

14. E-surveys—SurveyMonkey and Zoomerang

- Have you ever been marketed to through a survey? Let's take a tip from these marketers and ask our users to take a survey, then use the results in our own interests. In the old days, user satisfaction surveys could be very expensive, especially on the results input and collation and charts and graphs creation. But with online survey tools, it can be simple, fast, and cheap.

15. LinkedIn/Plaxo

- Most reporters are there—are you?
- Get yourself connected beyond libraries and into new realms.
- Check these out in a political context (e.g., for candidates, bond votes, propositions, etc.).

What can you offer with these 2.0 tools? First, you are information professionals and you'll need the format independence of this millennium. You'll not only need to know how to use each, but also how to search their trails, create alerts, develop search strategies, and provide advice. We can use this in the interest of the public good and education for our communities. Our organizations exist in a sociopolitical context and it's a valid use of our time to actively scan the environment for threats and opportunities everywhere.

Either way, 2.0 is another great opportunity that costs little and breaks organizational inertia. Are we ready for greater success?

Reasons for Promoting Your Library

1. Generate positive feelings about the library.
2. Increase the use of the library.
3. Increase awareness of current library programs and services.
4. Increase awareness of new library programs and services.
5. Cause an action (e.g., return overdue materials, register for an event, get a card).
6. Raise funds, get a new branch, support the library campaign, etc.
7. Achieve a political goal such as contact the mayor.

USING OP-EDS, LETTERS TO THE EDITOR, AND STATE OF THE LIBRARY REPORTS TO INFORM PUBLIC DEBATE

Chris Kertesz

EDITOR'S NOTE

What's the impact of the Internet on writing an op-ed or a letter to the editor?

Christine Kent, editor of Ragan's Media Relations Report, *says there are changing rules for landing in the opinion pages.*

"There's no doubt that e-mail and the Internet have created a lot more competition when you're trying to get an op-ed or a letter to the editor published. Where op-ed and letters editors might have received a few dozen submissions ten years ago, now they'll get hundreds—and in the case of big dailies like the New York Times *and the* Wall Street Journal—*thousands daily," she writes.*

Another strategy? Create your own blog content and podcasts, and you'll guarantee that your opinion will be published, she adds.

How important is timing? Since editors are often buried by submissions on hot topics, you must send out your letter quickly, sometimes within twenty-four hours.

"Another issue relating to speed is the media's short attention span for many news stories, given the drastically compressed news cycle for online publications. Something that's newsy at 10 a.m. may have totally lost its luster by 4 p.m. That may dictate which issue you take up in your op-ed or letter," writes Kent.

These days, more organizations are using viral e-mails, sent to supporters, members, and other key audiences, to sway public opinion, she writes.

Op-Eds

Op-eds are a lot of work, an investment of significant time and effort (as you'll see below) that may or may not pay off with publication and may or may not accomplish your goal of influencing public opinion.

So why bother?

What You Stand to Gain

Informed debate in a public forum is the lifeblood of democracy. Newspapers, magazines, and news and opinion websites usually go beyond reporting events and provide such a forum, often in their editorial and op-ed (from "opposite the editorial") pages. They use op-ed articles to give people with different points of view the opportunity to make their case and to ensure that their readers have access to diverse opinions on topics of importance to them.

Many media outlets actively seek outside experts to put local, state, national, and international events in perspective for their readers on the op-ed page, and most accept a limited number of unsolicited op-ed articles from contributors who demonstrate a grasp of the issue(s) and make an effective case for their point of view.

The op-ed page is a high-profile forum. Conventional news articles report the facts and aim to be objective. Op-ed pieces are also based on facts, but because they appear where they do it is understood that the writer is marshaling those facts in support of an argument. Op-ed pieces offer the public an opportunity to read and evaluate these arguments in a thoughtful way that is often not possible in the heat of a government hearing or sound-bite battle in the news.

That's why op-ed pieces are apt to be read and considered by members of the community who are in a position to influence public opinion—or help shape next year's library funding. And this is why an occasional op-ed piece is a valuable part of your arsenal of arguments.

First, publishing an op-ed piece is your opportunity to respond to a specific attack or situation. Has your library been criticized for some policy? Has someone questioned the value of what you are doing? Is your funding in jeopardy? Most librarians can answer *yes* to at least one of these questions. An op-ed piece is your chance to push back persuasively by making your case quickly and cogently and without interruption.

Second, an op-ed piece is your turn on the soapbox. Even if you are not responding to criticism, an op-ed piece is your chance to speak directly to the public and specifically to those who are in a position to help you by influencing public opinion or your prospects for funding. An op-ed can in fact be a response to a positive development—a follow-up to a positive story about a library program, for example, or an elaboration of the positive aspects of something like a new grant or service. You may not be looking for a specific result, but an op-ed can have a valuable, but hard-to-measure, long-term positive impact.

Finally, writing an op-ed helps you organize your thoughts on an important issue. The exercise of marshaling your facts and arguments to make your case or respond to an attack will leave you in better shape for the next round (and there will be a next round). You will have a firmer grasp of the issues. You'll have arguments ready to modify and roll out on another occasion. Perhaps most important, you will have been through the rigorous process of preparing your op-ed piece—flexed your writing muscles, so to speak. No matter what the fate of the article you submit, the process of writing, done right, is always fruitful in this way.

Rules to Refer Back To

Here are some basics to get you started:

Before you write, read. Many publications offer guidelines on length and other aspects of writing that are designed to help you shape an acceptable submission. These are usually available on the publication's website. Keep them handy and refer back to them as you write. You should also spend some time studying the publication in which you hope to publish your op-ed. Check out the competition by reading the op-eds that have been published and figuring out what they have in common. This is a thoughtful process; don't rush it. You have a lot of competition for this space, and one of the quickest ways to lose the contest is to be disqualified because you haven't done your homework.

Identify your audience (this is rule one for any kind of writing). Whose opinion are you trying to influence? Whose support are you looking for? Speak to them about issues that matter to them and speak in language they'll understand. If you stray into areas they don't care about, you'll lose them. If you address them in highfalutin terms, you'll come off as trying to sound superior. If you dumb it down too much, it may sound condescending.

Move quickly. Most op-eds are written in response to a current development in the world or a recent article or letter—or op-ed—in the target publication. The longer you wait to respond, the less timely your piece becomes and the less likely it will see the light of day. Be thoughtful and thorough, but don't dither.

Write tight! Use simple, declarative sentences. Choose your words with care. Make every word tell. Avoid long paragraphs. Use quotations only when they are more effective than paraphrasing and avoid partial quotes. As my city editor used to bark at me, about a half-century ago: "Write tight!"

> ### Tip
>
> Brush up your writing skills with some reading homework: William Strunk Jr. and E. B. White, *The Elements of Style,* available in many editions. You'll find no better guide to good writing.

Speak with authority. The op-ed should appear under the byline of a leader of your organization—CEO or president of the board, for example, or director of communications. That allows you to speak with authority. If you don't happen to be that leader (as is often the case), work closely with her or him to ensure that the two of you (and perhaps others) agree on the message you want to convey.

Get the reader's attention. Remember that this is not an essay or a term paper or a legal brief; no one is required to read it. That means you have to get people's attention quickly and arrange your material in a way that keeps them engaged. There are several ways to start an op-ed. The safest is probably to summarize, briefly, the issue and your view of it, then to list your arguments succinctly and in logical order, and then, at the end, to restate your conclusion. You can also begin by describing the personal experience of someone directly affected by the issue you're dealing with (anecdotal lead), but the story has to be relevant, compelling, and tellable in very few words. (Homework: Find an op-ed or two that you thought were particularly effective and try to figure out what made them so.)

Stick to your subject. You are probably writing about something you feel strongly about, and your piece may concern one aspect of a complex situation. Don't get carried away—no digressions, please!

Be positive. Only your partisans will cheer if you spend a lot of time running down the opposition. Don't waste your time preaching to the choir. Explain to the world why your position is the one to adopt rather than why the other guy is misinformed (or worse).

Listen to yourself. Good writing is conversational. Read your writing aloud, to yourself and/or to a colleague. If it doesn't sound convincing, it probably isn't, and your colleague may be able to tell you why. No thin skins are allowed in this business: once you put a word down on page or screen, it is no longer part of you. If you take suggestions or criticism personally, you are giving up a great resource.

Just the facts, ma'am (or sir). Op-eds are sometimes called *opinion pieces*, but you'll do better if you stick to the facts. Pick the few facts that will help you make your strongest case, and then make that case forcefully. Be selective; don't overdo it—too many facts will make your readers' eyes glaze over. Use humor sparingly and sarcasm even more so—the boomerang potential here is enormous.

. . . and make sure they're facts. Check your facts—and your grammar and spelling, including the spelling of people's names. This is vital. One error will undermine your credibility, and if you misspell someone's name, you acquire a lifelong detractor. (Hint: Ask a colleague or friend to run these checks for you; we all make errors, and we all tend to overlook our own errors.)

More don'ts: Avoid clichés. Avoid jargon. Avoid fancy words. Avoid long sentences. Avoid the passive. Don't try to be cute. And use exclamation marks sparingly!!!

Letters to the Editor

Letters to the editor are all of the above, boiled down to a few sentences. Timeliness and brevity are paramount. The competition for space is intense, and a letter that discusses a current issue or responds to a recent news article or op-ed succinctly is a stronger contender for that space.

Again, do your homework:

Read letters to the editor that have appeared in the publication you are writing to. What traits of writing do they have in common?

Read the publication's guidelines, if it offers them. The *New York Times,* for example, generally publishes only letters that respond to something that has appeared in the newspaper, while other papers open up the forum to a broader range of topics.

Follow the publication's letter style, which varies from one publication to another. This will show that you are a regular reader and will make your letter incrementally more attractive to an overburdened editor than a submission that needs a rewrite.

Thomas Feyer, who runs the letters to the editor section of the *New York Times,* offers tips to letter to the editor writers:

Every day at least 1,000 submissions, and often far more, pour in to the letters office by e-mail, fax or postal mail. We print an average of 15 letters a day. That means the competition is intense, to say the least. Many, many worthy letters never see print, and those that do cannot reflect all the topics of interest to readers.

What qualifies as a publishable letter to the editor? The answer is necessarily highly subjective. We are looking for a national (and often international) conversation about the issues of the day—big and not so big—as well as fresh, bright writing that stands out through its own charm. Timeliness is a must; brevity will improve your chances; stylishness and wit will win my heart . . .

Contrary to the impression of some readers, the letters page, unlike the editorials with which we share a home, does not have a political coloration of its own. We are eager to print all points of view—liberal, conservative and anything in between—expressed according to the rules of civil discourse. You are free to agree or disagree with the opinions expressed in the editorials, columns and op-ed articles, or with the articles in the news columns. We seek robust debate and strive for balance.

We welcome letters from all quarters, but especially from ordinary readers who have no titles after their names. Of course, we publish many writers speaking with authority in their areas of expertise, and letters from officeholders responding to criticism in these pages . . .

A few important ground rules: Letters should be kept to about 150 words. (Not enough space? Well, the Gettysburg Address was only about 250 words.) They should be exclusive to the Times *and respond to an article that appeared in the newspaper in the last week. In fact, writing by the next day is a good idea. Like other sections of the newspaper, the letters page seeks to be timely, so even a very good letter that arrives three days later may get passed over . . .*

Whether you are writing a letter to Mr. Feyer at the *New York Times* or to the newspaper that serves your community, keep this in mind: If at first you don't succeed in getting your letter published, by all means try, try again—but not too often. A reputation as a judicious contributor will serve you well.

Report on the State of Your Library

Libraries and librarians can also draw on and customize another ALA resource—the annual "State of America's Libraries" report—to inform their constituencies about developments relevant to their local libraries and reinforce your position as an important source of information for the media.

"The State of America's Libraries" (available at www .ala.org/ala/newspresscenter/mediapresscenter/press kits/2009stateofamericaslibraries/2009statehome .cfm) is what its title says, but it also seeks to foster read-

ing and literacy, support educational efforts, encourage productive use of the Internet, encourage defense of the right to read and other First Amendment rights, and contribute to community life and local economic development. The report focuses on areas that are likely to interest the media, such as basic factual data about libraries; trends in usage, construction, and funding; current issues; how libraries and librarians are keeping pace with rapidly developing information technologies; and libraries' efforts in the area of diversity and multicultural outreach.

The ALA report is national in scope, but it can also serve as a framework and starting point for a local "State of Anytown's Libraries" report. The executive summary can be especially useful in this regard; while you keep the focus on issues, data, and trends that are of interest locally, the executive summary can, in a few sentences, place the local facts in a national context. Beyond that, simply use what you need from the national report to provide a context for the data and developments in the local report.

For example, if you choose to highlight funding for local school libraries and library media specialists, you can draw on the national "State of America's Libraries" report to note that, "For the first time ever, funding for school libraries and the school library media specialists who staff them is declining," and go on to cite the National Center for Education Statistics data in the report. (Note that any local report should probably begin with material on the local situation, then turn to the national report and its content for purposes of comparison—e.g., "Our funding for local school libraries and library media specialists remained flat last year—which is still better than the national average, which declined.")

Another possibility: A section on local circulation and library-use data could refer to the national report, which noted that, "Americans continue to check out more than two billion items each year from their public libraries. . . . The average user takes out seven-plus

> ## Tip
>
> Spruce up your report. Use Microsoft Word, Excel, or other software to generate simple graphics based on your data; they'll add impact to your report and make its pages easier on the eye.

books a year, but patrons also go to their libraries to borrow DVDs, learn new computer skills, conduct job searches, and participate in the activities of local community organizations." What are the comparable local numbers? What kinds of factors are worth mentioning in the local report that might not have been relevant in the national report?

If you have issues that are unique to the local library situation, you can deal with them using the national report as a template.

You can post your local report on your website, make hard copies available in the library, and pass them along to your Friends group, if you have one. Send or hand-deliver copies to local media outlets, opinion-makers, funders, and funding prospects—a concise "State of Anytown's Libraries" report can make an excellent leave-behind piece for development work.

In any case, get your library's story out there where people can see it! It's a great story, and it's getting better all the time.

5

COOKING UP CULTURE

Michael Steinmacher

EDITOR'S NOTE

One of the best ways to get patrons to the library may be through their stomachs. Many libraries have used the culinary arts to entice the public to visit and use their services. Here the Kentucky Free Public Library whips up a soufflé of programs to whet the appetite of customers. At the end of the chapter, enjoy some great examples of what libraries from around the country are doing, including an edible moveable feast to support Banned Books Week.

There are only a few things in life that quickly create a sense of camaraderie and fellowship among strangers. One of them is an everyday event called eating. Whether it's a group of parishioners at a church potluck or coworkers sitting down around the lunchroom table, there is something universal about the effect of food and the bond that it creates among people. The library—a place where people of varying needs and wants gather—can have a similar bonding effect.

In an effort to heighten community cultural and educational awareness, the Iroquois branch of Louisville (Kentucky) Free Public Library (LFPL) whipped up a menu of programs in January 2005 called "Cooking Up Culture" that sought to capture people's interest through this unique gastronomic bond. The goal was to educate people about today's multicultural world through the culinary arts, to heighten awareness of the library's overall work, and to create community partnerships with local organizations and businesses.

The original concept was to have an in-house chef-in-residence. The idea was then developed and expanded by adding two components: overall programs designed to educate patrons about today's multicultural world, and the support of local businesses.

At the time the series was being developed, library staff was unaware of a similar program of the same name at Boston University. While both programs focused on cultural education, the LFPL series differed from Boston's in that Louisville's emphasis was on heightening awareness of library services, building community relationships, and providing free programming.

LFPL's program was part of the system's larger international initiatives, which are designed to reach out to the community's growing global population, while simultaneously reconnecting with its traditional patron base. It was funded by a grant from the Louisville-based CE and S Foundation and primarily based at the Iroquois branch.

Library staff sought to give the series greater depth and to enrich participant experiences by actively pursuing a philosophy of community librarianship. Series contributors included restaurateurs, the city's Office for International Affairs, grocery stores, community groups, the Friends of the Library chapter, and the local high school. Although the cooking programs served as a foundation for the series, programming was expanded to focus on such topics as travel, the arts, entertainment, and the humanities.

Mixing the Melting Pot

Key to the overall success of the series was identifying and retaining a local chef. Nancy Russman, a twenty-year veteran of the Louisville restaurant scene, was recruited to fill this role. Russman and library staff decided to host ten two-hour programs over a six-month period that would focus on specific regions or countries and include discussion about the geographic, religious, historical, and linguistic influences upon each culture's choice of food.

In addition to choosing regions that were representative of the community's international makeup, consideration was given as to how and where civilization developed and spread throughout the world. The series began with the Middle East (specifically the countries of Iran and Iraq) and "traveled" to East Africa, West Africa, India, Vietnam, Eastern Europe, Germany, Cuba, Mexico, and the Caribbean.

Each program followed roughly the same format and allowed for the participation of sixty people at a time. Russman discussed the culture of the evening and provided a general overview of the influences involved in shaping the particular country's cuisine choices. Program presenters, including restaurateurs recruited by Metro Louisville's Office for International Affairs and other guests representing agencies serving specific cultural groups, were then introduced. Russman's

humor and quick wit enlivened each event and created a festive environment that prompted program participants to engage in lively banter with presenters.

As the discussion proceeded, Russman prepared dishes consistent with the culture of the evening's focus and engaged restaurateurs by asking questions about the culture they represented. The dishes were prepared using authentic ingredients purchased at or donated by local businesses. At one of the programs, questions arose about the items necessary for the preparation of the dishes. The manager of the local Valumarket grocery store was present as an invited guest and was able to answer inquiries ranging from the availability of the ingredients to the shelf life of items used in the recipe.

Expanding the Dining Experience

Because the program was designed as much more than a cooking class, specific efforts were made to promote library resources. Russman used and recommended library materials during the programs. Print and audiovisual materials were available for immediate checkout. Brochures for each program included a bibliography, lists of local businesses serving those interested in the featured culture, a list of program partners, and basic geographic information. Library staff served as program hosts and was available to answer questions.

Although the original audience of the program series was intended to be traditional patrons, the actual attendance was a mix of near-capacity programs with ethically and racially diverse audiences representing a cross section of the community. As one component of the library's larger work to reach its international and traditional communities, "Cooking Up Culture" was an enormous success.

APPENDIX
Additional Tasty Examples of Food as a Promotional Tool

By Mark R. Gould

Other libraries are cooking up great ways to use the culinary arts to promote their services:

One library celebrated Banned Books Week 2008 by holding "an edible book event." Susan Franklin of Hastings College Perkins Library in Nebraska reports that Sigma Tau Delta, the honorary English society, invited participants to gather on the library's porch at noon to "Consume a Moveable Feast" of cooked dishes and baked goods that resembled the covers of banned books, conveyed in some way the content of banned books, or cleverly played with the words in banned books titles:

> *Approximately forty-five participants dined on sixteen tasty creations, ranging from shell pasta salad* (Brighton Beach Memoirs); *a smorgasbord of grapes, violet gumdrops, eggplant, purple M&Ms and jelly beans for* The Color Purple; *an artfully wrought cake reproduction of the famous* The Great Gatsby *cover; and a cake depiction of* Bridge to Terabithia, *complete with a blue Jell-O river and a licorice bridge. While devouring the banned books, members of the group took turns reading aloud from banned books. No one had the heart to mar the work of art that was* The Great Gatsby *by cutting it, so the cake was put on a twenty-four-hour silent auction, which netted $30 for Sigma Tau Delta and benefited the Introduction to Literature class that was lucky to share it in class.*

Franklin added, "Our celebration took Sir Francis Bacon's famous words quite literally: 'Some books are to be tasted, others to be swallowed, and some few to be chewed and digested.'"

Canton Public Library in Michigan offered programming called "Connect with Your Neighbors" that highlighted various ethnic groups in the community. "Last year, for our annual Chinese New Year celebration, we had a chef come to the library and do simple wok cooking demonstrations with samples for the audience. It was very popular and delicious, too. We provided copies of the recipes for the attendees as well as some general information about Chinese New Year.

The year before, we did a Chinese fair with bonsai demos, calligraphy demos, tai chi demos and more. These diversity programs are very popular and food always attracts a crowd," says Marcia Barker of Canton Public Library.

Susan Di Mattia says that the Friends of Ferguson Library, Stamford, Connecticut's public library, hosts an annual book and author luncheon in the spring, featuring three authors. Authors are invited to submit their favorite recipes to be included in a cookbook, which is sold in the Friends bookstore.

Roberta Barton of the Fresno County Public Library says her library has sponsored several Big Read events, one featuring *The Joy Luck Club*. "We created a cooking program with our job services outreach librarian [Bernice Kao] demonstrating several Chinese recipes and cooked the dishes right there in the library. We contacted our local cable provider and they produced a cooking demonstration of the program in their studios complete with a kitchen (just like Martha Stewart or Rachel Ray). The second half of the cable program featured several library staff gathered around the table enjoying her food and discussing *The Joy Luck Club*. I christened the program, 'Kao Can Cook!' Comcast is still broadcasting this show today."

According to Pamela Reeder of Murrell Memorial Library at Missouri Valley College in Marshall, Missouri, the library held a successful culinary program to mark Black History Month. The school's associate professor of anthropology presented a lecture entitled, "Soul Food: An Archaeological Perspective of African American Identity." Soul food recipes for tasting during the lecture were prepared by library staff and included corn bread, sweet potato biscuits, black-eyed peas, collard greens, fried chicken, grits, and jambalaya. The program was free and open to the public.

Tying food to programs works especially well for teen and intergenerational programming, says Joan Cales of Winfield (Kansas) Public Library. "As part of the programming for the Smithsonian exhibit 'Between Fences,' our teen group hosted an event that showcased food that highlighted the different ethnicities in the community. We also had a series several years ago for teens that studied different world cultures. We have a halfway joking motto here—feed them and they will come," she said.

Finally, Amanda Ghobrial of the West Chicago Public Library District in Illinois asked this question: "How can you bring together generationally disparate groups of people (who are important to each other, but don't fully realize it)? I'm talking about the library board, the Friends of the Library, and, the members of the Young Adult Advisory Council. You can do it with food!" Ghobrial says dinners have enabled the groups to realize they have common library goals. "Throughout the years the variety of countries represented has been incredible: the American South; the Middle East; Ireland; England; Germany, etc. The dinner is usually around Thanksgiving—the perfect time for a feast. The teens decorate the Library Program Room, transforming it into an elegant dining room including linens, (fake) candlelight, and soothing music. This annual, greatly anticipated event has always been an exceedingly positive experience for the teens and their guests," she says.

6

HARNESS A CELEBRITY BRAND AND CREATE EFFECTIVE PRINT PUBLIC SERVICE ANNOUNCEMENTS

Mark R. Gould

Cybill Shepherd taught me the power of a celebrity's brand.

Here's how it happened: In the mid-1980s, I worked as the communications director for the Chicago Lung Association, then an affiliate of the American Lung Association. One day, a letter from headquarters landed on my desk with an announcement that Cybill Shepherd, the star of the popular TV show *Moonlighting* with Bruce Willis, had been named the organization's national spokesperson of their Christmas Seals campaign.

Ms. Shepherd, I learned, had agreed to let the Lung Association and its affiliates use her image in print public service announcements, record radio public service announcements (PSAs), and provide some great quotes about lung health that we could use in our local public relations efforts.

When the media received the materials, there was a lot of interest. Many radio stations aired Shepherd's PSAs. But they wanted more.

What they wanted was to interview Cybill. Unfortunately she was not available to make in-studio TV appearances, conduct phone interviews, or just about anything else in the category of personal appearances. However, I soon learned that some access is a lot better than none at all.

No Time? Let the "Brand" Do It

Celebrities only need to make a little time available to help a nonprofit organization, and let the power of their "brand" do the rest. A radio PSA, a quote, or a photo op can be turned into a publicity campaign with a large return on their time investment.

When I checked out the American Lung Association's previous Christmas Seals celebrity supporters, I learned that they had accessed the following celebrity "brands": Jacqueline Kennedy Onassis (believe it or not), Bob Hope, Rock Hudson, Johnny Bench, and Pearl Bailey, all of whom had helped the cause in much the same way as Cybill Shepherd.

The model has been so successful that the Lung Association continues to use it today; Olympic skater Kristi Yamaguchi, who won television's popular *Dancing with the Stars* competition in 2008, is the latest celebrity to lend her image to the cause.

There's a lesson here for libraries, and the good news is that you don't have to start tracking down celebrities or negotiating with agents. Libraries around the country can piggyback on American Library Association celebrity tie-ins by connecting to the national efforts of ALA and its units or those of state associations and chapters.

Each year, the ALA Public Information Office works with a well-known figure to serve as the honorary chair of National Library Week and Library Card Sign-up Month. George Lopez, Julie Andrews, Jamie Lee Curtis, and sports figures Kareem Abdul-Jabbar, Olympic gold medalist basketball player Candace Parker, and NFL quarterback Ben Roethlisberger have lent their brand to ALA. We often contact the figure's publicist and work out an agreement that gives us an opportunity to take a photo and record PSAs that we then use in our promotions. Not all celebrities are willing to do all of these activities, so we mix and match.

When you check the ALA website, you'll find that print PSAs featuring the honorary chair can be customized with your library's logo and contact information. You can then pitch local media to donate space and run the PSA; you may also find radio PSAs, sometimes television PSAs, and even a podcast or two. In addition, the content can be used on your library website, in newsletters or fliers, as signage, and more.

ALA places the print PSAs in national magazines and generates millions of dollars in donated ad space in national magazines. PSAs featuring Julie Andrews and Kareem Abdul-Jabbar were published in *Entertainment Weekly*, *Sports Illustrated*, *O*, *USA Today*, *Redbook*, *Parents*, and *U.S. News & World Report* and generated more than $2 million in donated ad space in 2008.

How to Develop Your Own Celebrity PSAs

Or you can develop your own public service announcement campaign.

First, you need a celebrity—the mayor, a community leader, or a former celebrity resident. Then organize a photo shoot and get a great image. Select a pro-fessional photographer who has experience creating high-level portraits. Have your designer create a PSA template that you can send to media or businesses in the community; your designer will have to be able to provide a file that reflects the print specifications, or specs, of the publication.

Be creative—and make sure you insist that the celebrity signs up for a library card if she or he doesn't have one!

Ask the local media to publish the print PSA in the community newspaper; invite other organizations to promote your messages by publishing them in their newsletters and placing them on their websites. You'll need to develop a web icon for websites—and don't forget to print the piece and post it all over your library, drop it off at city hall, and ask local businesses to display it.

> ▶ **Tip**
>
> Make sure you give print media enough time to find a spot to run your print PSAs. Regional and local monthly publications will need ninety to one hundred and twenty days' notice.

Jené O'Keefe Trigg, managing director at Pro-Media Communications, offers these tips:

1. Create a visually appealing ad that appeals to a diverse audience. Also create a banner ad for websites.

2. Keep the narrative to a minimum—but be sure to have a call to action, such as "Visit our website."

3. Start pitching a minimum three months in advance.

4. Work with a graphic designer that is able to *quickly* resize your ad based on a magazine's specifications.

A small investment of time and energy can generate a dramatic increase in publicity for your library.

Ready to get started? Larry Bloom of ATI Graphics (www.atigraphics.com) has worked closely with ALA on national PSA projects. Here's his list of best-practice tips for working with graphic files for print PSAs:

1. *Do NOT edit original photo files.* Preserve the original images and other graphics that will be used in the print PSA and do your work on copies. Saving changes to the size, resolution, or format of the original digital photo or graphic image may limit its future use. Always work on copies of files so that in case you need to revert to the file's initial state, you can simply refer back to the original file.

2. *Don't depend on your monitor for proper color and exposure.* If you are building your print PSA using a photo image provided by a professional photographer or stock-photo house, chances are the color is balanced properly and the exposure is correct. Since all monitors are calibrated differently—or more likely not calibrated by the user at all—an image that appears too dark, too light, too magenta, etc., on your screen may in fact be just right. Modifying it might produce a poorer image.

Whenever possible, when working with publications or printers, get a hard-copy proof subject to your approval so you can see exactly what your PSA will look like in print. If a hard copy is not available or time constraints do not allow for this step, make sure your point of contact understands your concern that the color and exposure be accurate and that they should let you know ASAP if any adjustments to the image are necessary.

3. *Save your document repeatedly as you work through the design process.* Remember to save your document periodically as you work. That way, if your computer crashes, the power is interrupted or a reboot is needed for any reason, your file will have the most recent changes when you're up and running again, and little or no work will have been lost.

4. *Use vector graphics whenever possible.* Unlike raster (bitmap) graphics, vector graphics can be resized, large or small, without compromising image quality. Having your text, clip art, and logos in vector format will make easy work of resizing a letter-sized print PSA to a poster.

5. *Create your design for print, even if the PSA is initially intended for use on the Web.* A print-quality photo layout should be 300 dpi (dots per inch) at 100 percent of the document size. You may be creating a layout to be displayed on the Web—which only requires 72 dpi—but you should not limit the usefulness of your PSA. Create your original document at "print resolution" and reformat it for the Web upon exporting the layout or saving a copy of the file. This way, if you subsequently discover that a print version is needed, you won't have to start from scratch. Rule of thumb: You can always resize *down* without losing image and graphic quality, but resizing *up* will usually compromise the quality of the final product.

6. *Always keep a "layered" version of your final design.* If you are applying text or graphics to a photo image in Photoshop, be sure to save an "unflattened" version of the file. Once you save and close a file that has been flattened (all layers combined into a single, compressed layer), you will not be able to edit the text or other graphics applied over the photo. Essentially, it all becomes part of the photo image.

7. *Find out the correct mechanical specifications of the output device, publication, or print house* before *you begin your work.* You might waste a lot of time and money if your print PSA document has not been properly prepared. Every print house and publication has unique mechanical specs such as *bleed, trim,* and *safe area.* Two magazines may offer identical ad sizes, but the required specifications most likely will *not* be compatible. There is not necessarily an industry standard on which you can depend.

Depending on their software and hardware, printers and publications have different requirements for the type of file you can send them. For example, many require PDF files saved in CMYK color format.

Cybill Shepherd inspired me to better understand the power of a celebrity brand. I hope this piece has inspired you to build visibility for your library by connecting to ALA spokespeople or creating your own campaign with local celebrities.

APPENDIX
Reaching Out to the Community with the READ Program

By Steve Zalusky

The American Library Association launched its READ poster series in 1979. Based on a simple yet universally appealing message—READ—these posters have become a beloved cultural icon, used to promote literacy in libraries and classrooms all over the world. You probably already display ALA's celebrity READ posters in your library; in this appendix you'll find some creative ideas for spreading the gospel of libraries and reading—as well as promoting your own library—using READ posters that you create yourself.

It was Peggy Barber, now co-owner and director of Library Communication Strategies, who advanced the idea of the READ poster when she was ALA's associate executive director of communications. (Barber credits the late Betty Stearns, vice president of Public Relations Board, Inc., with hatching the idea for the posters.) "When we started the public information office, we made the decision that we wanted to focus more on external communication in promoting libraries and not just providing media relations about the American Library Association," she said. The concept of the READ posters grew from that desire to help you promote your library.

Today, ALA Graphics employs the successful formula of selecting iconic celebrities and characters who will be most effective in promoting libraries, literacy, and reading, weighing such factors as diversity, a celebrity's current following, and his or her ability to reach different age groups. In order to learn what fans, librarians, and readers want to see on a poster, ALA Graphics conducts extensive research, closely following popular culture—who's hot in magazines, in movies, and on TV, and paying attention to feedback from customers about whom they would like to see featured on a poster.

Celebrities donate their time and their image and choose their own book—any book except one they've written. Beginning with the first poster, which featured Mickey Mouse, the honor roll of stars has grown to include popular fictional characters such as Miss Piggy and Yoda, famous sporting figures such as Shaquille O'Neal and Danica Patrick, film and TV stars such as Orlando Bloom, Morgan Freeman, and Dakota Fanning, and musicians such as Yo-Yo Ma and Ani DiFranco, among many others.

ALA created the READ CD in response to requests from individual libraries that wanted to make their own posters for more community-based promotion. Using the READ CD, libraries, schools, and other nonprofit organizations can build on the success of the READ program by creating their own posters that emulate the iconic celebrity READ posters, featuring local celebrities, politicians, library staff and patrons, and other members of the community. In addition to posters, some users create bookmarks, T-shirt iron-ons, stickers, buttons, pins, name tags, trading cards, stationery, reading log books, and more.

Tips on Using the READ CDs to Market Your Library

ALA provides the ingredients on the CD—it's up to you to provide the creativity. Here are some suggestions garnered from libraries around the country:

- Put librarians and teachers on READ posters to promote the new school year; place the posters on the door to greet students on their first day of school.
- Create bookmarks, buttons, pins, or name tags.
- Get local politicians to pose for READ posters. This win-win strategy not only provides publicity for your civic representatives, but brings your library to their attention as well.
- If you have a nationally recognized celebrity in your community, ask her or him to pose for a READ poster. For example, Sue Grafton, a Kentucky-based writer, posed for a READ poster for the Kentucky Public Library Association.
- Feature members of your community who are notable for civic activities.
- Feature super readers: sponsor a reading contest and make a poster of the student or patron who reads the most books.

Case Studies

Here are several examples of libraries that developed their own distinctive series of READ posters:

One library that has capitalized on the READ software's potential is the Skokie Public Library in Skokie, Illinois. "It is a great public relations effort," said library director Carolyn Anthony. She said the library was able to convince a wide range of political officials to pose for READ posters. The list included the mayor and local state representatives, a congresswoman and both of Illinois's senators, one of whom ultimately became president of the United States—Barack Obama.

The elected officials each hung their own READ poster in their office, which added to the public relations value, because, as Anthony points out, "as various constituencies have come in to [legislators' offices to] make their pitches, they'll see this library poster there. How great is that?"

Anthony said that the Skokie program was soon expanded to include notable people in the community, including representatives from some of the ethnic groups that live there. At first the posters were displayed in the library, but their appeal proved so contagious that they were placed in park district facilities, a nearby performing arts center, the village hall, and even some businesses including the grocery store down the street and a couple of restaurants. "Someone from the Chinese community appeared on the poster hanging in the Chinese restaurant," she added. "The idea was that it's kind of a further extension of what we do with our library signs in many languages, which is a way to reach out and say, 'You're welcome here.'"

Anthony said the posters have definitely had a positive impact on foot traffic at her library, which means more people coming to attend programs and use computers, as well as using the library's other services.

Another organization that has had success with customized READ posters is the Kentucky Department of Libraries and Archives. Judith Gibbons, former director of field services, said the Kentucky libraries are "always looking for a good hook to try to educate our elected officials about the importance of public libraries in the state."

The Public Library Association legislative committee in Kentucky found that hook when they hung READ posters featuring state legislators in the tunnel that connects the capitol and the state office building—and, in the process, struck marketing and promotional gold. The positioning of the posters proved ideal, because the tunnel sees a lot of traffic between the governor's office and the two houses of the legislature.

"[This tunnel] is very helpful because we can really attract people's attention there," noted Gibbons. "In the winter people are a captive audience; they have to use the tunnel. So you have the governor's staff, you have legislators, you have lobbyists, you have the common folk that are coming to the capitol, you've got school tours," she said. "In other words, what better way to reach people about the value of libraries—and in the process flatter the elected and appointed officials who appeared on the posters? We got tremendous results from the constituents and also from the legislators and the governor's office."

Raymond Santiago, director of the Miami-Dade Public Library System in Florida, said READ posters displayed in his library highlighted influential decision makers who might have some impact on the system's future.

"We used them really to highlight our elected officials, our mayor, and our county commission members," he said, adding that poster subjects were e-mailed the files, so they could use them in their own e-newsletters. "At one point, we made small cards for them that they could distribute." Connecting libraries with people in government gives them a feeling of ownership in the libraries, he said.

For more information on the READ program, visit the ALA store at www.alastore.ala.org, where you can see all available celebrity READ posters and other READ incentives and learn more about the trademarked READ CDs, including creative ways to use them to enhance your library's outreach. Also check out the READ CD blog at http://readcd .ala.org/blog/, for more ideas about how to use the READ CD.

7

SAVVY OUTREACH TACTICS, SPECIAL EVENTS FOCUS THE MEDIA'S ATTENTION ON YOUR MESSAGE

Jené O'Keefe Trigg

EDITOR'S NOTE
Communicators face significant challenges obtaining the attention of the news media these days for a variety of reasons. According to the PEW Research State of the News Media 2008 report, the amount of content the news media devotes to domestic issues is shrinking. The report says, "Consider the list of the domestic issues that each filled less than a single percent of the news hole: education, race, religion, transportation, the legal system, housing, drug trafficking, gun control, welfare, Social Security, aging, labor, abortion, and more."

The report also states, "A related trait is a tendency to move on from stories quickly. On breaking news events—the Virginia Tech massacre or the Minneapolis bridge collapse were among the biggest—the media flooded the zone but then quickly dropped underlying story lines about school safety and infrastructure. And newer media seem to have an even narrower peripheral vision than older media. Cable news, talk radio (and also blogs) tend to seize on top stories (often polarizing ones) and amplify them. The Internet offers the promise of aggregating ever more sources, but its value still depends on what those originating sources are providing. Even as the media world has fragmented into more outlets and options, reporting resources have shrunk."

Jené O'Keefe Trigg, a veteran media relations professional, has put together some tips for communicators on how to work effectively in this changing—and shrinking—news environment.

Reporters, editors, and producers are always looking for good story ideas, particularly stories that have a direct impact on their readers. To generate interest in subjects that will resonate with your supporters and will help you influence public opinion, consider the following tactics:

Find out which reporters have covered literacy and library issues in the past. In addition to those who cover these issues, target op-ed contributors and columnists. Be sure to include radio producers and university and public broadcasting media, as well as weekly community papers. Make a list of media contacts with e-mail and phone information.

Gather relevant information and tailor it to your community and state. While facts and figures are important, it is always more powerful to put a human face on statistics, with real life examples (particularly someone from your city, state, or community).

Target your outreach to coincide with newsworthy events, such as new legislation, funding cuts, or a particularly interesting event at your library. Timeliness is always key in the news business. Connect outreach efforts to specific news hooks to make your pitch as newsworthy as possible. Keep in mind, however, that if there are no relevant new stories, it can still be helpful to send materials as an "fyi." By giving reporters background materials, you can present yourself as a resource when the appropriate news story surfaces.

Submit—or get one of your supporters to submit—an op-ed to your local newspaper. Call the newspaper to determine the necessary length, deadline and preferred submission format (e-mail or fax). Make sure to include information in the op-ed specific to your community and/or state. (See chapter 4.)

Monitor your local media. If you see an appropriate news story that fails to mention your main messages, contact the reporter and give him or her the pertinent facts. Use a helpful, not critical, tone so that they are likely to call on you as an expert for future pieces on related topics

Schedule and conduct an editorial board meeting. Every daily newspaper has an editorial board, which can comprise one to a dozen people. As a citizen in the community, you can contact the editorial board and attempt to persuade it to take a position on behalf of your library. To do this, begin by calling your local newspaper and asking for the editorial board; then ask to schedule a meeting. Give them a quick sense of what's in it for them; let them know why, in this busy news environment, they benefit from meeting with a library spokesperson.

Write and *call.* Journalists are used to getting a lot of e-mails, so make sure your subject line is short and to the point to ensure it gets noticed. Don't be flowery in your language. You can submit either a pitch letter (which allows you to get a bit more in-depth, and can also be used on stories that are not related to breaking news) or a press release (used for breaking news—an event, a change in leadership, etc.). But most important, call. Make a personal connection with the journalist. Call and call again—they are not easy to reach. Leave some messages (but not every time you call if you are able to call frequently) and when you reach them, be gracious. Ask them if they are on deadline. Then, tell them your main message right away. Offer to provide them with any data, stories, etc., that they would need to run the story you want them to run.

Special events can also be a great tactic to introduce your library or a new program at your library to your community, the media, and your supporters. By bringing together people in one room you can get your messages out to a large group at one time.

A traditional press conference is not recommended unless you have a major news development that has reporters jamming your phone lines. Create an event that will appeal to a wider range of audiences to ensure attendance—including media.

Planning Your Event

Some of the actions described below will need to be done simultaneously. For example, you need to determine the participants, the location, and the date as soon as you get started. However, these details may only come together as you get closer to the event date. Keep your staff/donors/friends/development committee abreast of the event status on a regular basis and remind everyone that flexibility is important.

The Space

The event can be held in an indoor or outdoor space. Plan on having a space that accommodates fewer people than you think you will have so that it looks full no matter how many people attend. It may be best if the space has no permanent fixtures so that you can set it up as desired.

A Few Ideas for Format

For a panel discussion or stage presentation, use a stage with a dais—where your speakers may sit and either speak as a panel, or stand and go to podium to make their remarks. If you have a stage, be sure to have steps or a ramp—either near your podium or on the side of the stage. On and around the stage you may want to place a podium with a sign attached to the front that highlights the name of your library and a large banner hanging on the back of the stage that will be captured in video or photos. Also think of any other visual elements that might add impact, such as signs on easels or images on a screen.

A coffee meet and greet or afternoon reception is a more casual event where people are encouraged to mingle. You should have a podium centrally located for the presentation portion of your event—where key speakers could give remarks with guests standing or sitting around them.

An interactive workshop event could highlight a new program at your library and enable guests to have a hands-on experience.

Room Setup

The room setup may include the following:

Seats: The size of your space will help you to determine the number of chairs to set up. Fewer seats than people is always recommended. A space of approximately ten feet should be left between the stage and the chairs, so there is plenty of space for people to walk up to the stage.

Microphone: You might set up a microphone on a stand for attendees to use when they ask questions.

Informational table: Consider having a table with informational tools such as press materials, brochures, newsletters—and a sign-up sheet. You may also want to put key materials on the chairs to ensure people see and take them.

Press sign-in area: This can be a table, or one end of the informational table, that has a press sign-in form and press kits.

Date and Location

As you consider the date for your event, make sure the date you've selected isn't the date of a big city or state-wide event that will steal your thunder. Some of the other questions you may want to ask yourself:

Will the event be outside? If so, is the weather a factor? If the event is outside (whether or not you have a legislator involved), you'll probably need to get a local permit to hold it there. Start early to secure this. If you have never gained a permit and you have no legislator to expedite the paperwork, ask your colleagues if someone has experience with this, or go to your local police precinct to start the ball rolling.

Should you hold the event at your library or at the state capitol if it is pegged to legislation?

Will the legislature be in session on the day you're planning your event?

Is there a supportive, high-profile individual or elected official who would cosponsor the event? If you think there is, you will need to check with that person's staff very early on so that you can determine their availability and their willingness to be part of the event.

Can you collaborate on the event with other libraries or groups in your community?

Participants and Speakers

Every library or library community has its own public and private funding streams, supporters, partners, etc., and so it will be up to each of you to determine who will be willing and able to participate in the event.

It's also important to let the event take shape as you go—because you may not know from the beginning exactly what it will look like. Here are some examples and pointers to use as you work through your planning.

Invite special guests/dignitaries—those who are supportive and with whom you are developing a relationship.

Invite a wide array of library users—an adult literacy student, business owner, parent or child—to tell their story about how the library has benefited them.

Invite key library leaders from your city and state such as the state librarian, or representatives from your school, academic, and public libraries to speak.

Invite national ALA spokespeople to attend and speak at your event. Invite them to speak to media before, during, and after the event as well.

The Program

Once you have a good idea of who is committed to speak, begin to work out the order of the program. Visualize where people will be positioned while speaking and what action they will take when they are finished making remarks. This possible program sequence offers a guideline:

- music
- welcome by board president (two to three minutes)
- short personal stories by three to five library users (each one minute or less)
- remarks by VIPs (e.g., elected officials, committee chairs; two minutes each)

- more short personal stories by three to five more library users (each one minute or less)
- wrap-up with Q and A

Media Attendance

If possible, send personal invitations, followed up by phone calls, to key journalists you hope will attend. Journalists like the opportunity to interview key library figures at the event so that they can get the most out of the event in terms of coverage. Find out their needs in advance as much as possible. For example, is someone coming with a camera crew? A photographer? Does someone want to live-blog from the front row?

For the day of the event, have a list of journalists you expect to attend, as well as a sheet that unexpected media representatives can use to sign in. If you expect a large number of journalists, have a separate sign-in area for them to check in and gather any press materials you want them to have.

Expect alternative media to attend and decide in advance how you will handle them. It is a good idea to establish criteria ahead of time for admitting bloggers, newsletter editors, and writers for in-house publications, to help with any space constraints you may have. Consider welcoming anyone who specializes in your issues and who can reach your target audiences.

8

STRENGTHEN COMMUNICATION THROUGH A NATIONAL PUBLIC AWARENESS INITIATIVE

Megan Humphrey

Unifying communication has brought renewed energy to library promotions through the American Library Association's popular Campaign for America's Libraries. Today, thousands of libraries of all types use the campaign's @ your library brand.

This national public awareness campaign was a response to the challenges libraries faced toward the end of the twentieth century. Popular institutions, but ones that were often taken for granted, libraries were rooted then—as they are now—in nearly every school, campus, and community. However, they were not visible and made news primarily when they were under siege. Libraries were unique institutions, paying a unique public role, but they were under increasing pressure from bookstores and the Internet to define what is unique about them.

To highlight the value of libraries and librarians, help update the image of librarians, bring renewed energy to the promotion of libraries and libraries, and unify communication, the Campaign for America's Libraries was launched in Washington, D.C., in 2001. From the beginning, the campaign has generated positive publicity for libraries on a national basis, and for the work of libraries in communities all over America.

A Library of Resources for Libraries

To make the case on behalf of the value of libraries and librarians, the campaign offers a library of resources that libraries, librarians, and library supporters can draw on to educate the public about their value. The campaign brand was developed to be adaptable to every situation. ALA uses the @ your library brand in national initiatives to focus positive public attention on libraries and librarians, while libraries of all types all across the nation—and around the world—use @ your library to promote their local programs.

Communicators continue to respond enthusiastically to the @ your library brand; that's because it is customizable and available for all libraries to download and use at no cost. The campaign responds to the local, individualized needs of libraries large and small; urban, suburban, and rural; public and private; and those serving primary, secondary, and higher education students. Useful, cost-effective, and peer-tested ideas and materials have been tailored for specific use by individual ALA members and others, enabling them to capitalize on the existing high level of public support for libraries and ALA's large network of friends and advocates.

Here are some examples of how different types of libraries tapped into the campaign resources and how your library can connect to the Campaign for America's Libraries.

National Library Week: Local Themes, Local Campaigns

National Library Week is one of the most popular uses of the @ your library brand. During this annual week-long celebration in April, libraries use a single theme to promote the value of libraries in their communities. The @ your library brand has been an integral part of the National Library Week promotion since 2001; the 2007 National Library Week theme, for example, was "Come together @ your library." Here are some examples that may inspire future efforts in your community to celebrate National Library Week:

In Clarks Summit, Pennsylvania, the Abington Community Library used "Come together @ your library" to celebrate cultural heritage; the library hosted events celebrating Russia, Greece, England, and Spain, culminating in a popular international game night.

The Maricopa County Library District in Phoenix, Arizona, partnered with a local theater company to present an original stage adaptation of "Tomás and the Library Lady," by Pat Mora, a story that literally shows how one can "Change your world @ your library." The play was presented at thirty local schools and the district's librar-

ies, reaching nearly thirty-three thousand children. The library coupled the performances with a library card sign-up campaign. Every child attending a performance received a bilingual brochure promoting the library and encouraging them to sign up for a library card.

In Houston, Minnesota (population 1,500), more than forty volunteers wrapped a donated library building that resembled "a drab military bunker" in a mural whose central feature was "Find it @ your library!" The Friends of the Houston Public Library received the 2004 Baker and Taylor/FOLUSA-sponsored award for the best use of the @ your library brand and campaign materials.

The National Literary Society of the Deaf (NLSD) used National Library Week and "Come together @ your library" as a springboard for announcing the addition of an NLSD home page on the Friends of Libraries for Deaf Action website and the development of a new directory, "Deaf people work @ your library."

> ▶ Tip
>
> Create a winning entry: Take a look at the guidelines for the Scholastic Library Publishing National Library Week grant competition. The grant awards funds annually for the best public awareness campaign tied to National Library Week. Information is available on the ALA website at www.ala.org/ala/aboutala/hqops/pio/natlibraryweek/nlwgrant.cfm.

Library Card Sign-up Month

The launch of the Public Library Association's "Smartest Card" campaign in 2004 provided Library Card Sign-up Month with a theme that all public libraries have used to promote the most important card in everyone's wallet. By connecting local initiatives to the theme "The Smartest Card. Get it. Use it. @ your library"—public libraries nationwide were able to promote local and regional library-card campaigns and benefit from the media outreach efforts done on behalf of the initiative at the national level.

The State Library of North Carolina, for example, spearheaded a statewide "Smartest Card" campaign to promote Library Card Sign-up Month in 2004, a campaign which continued through 2008. The effort resulted in an impressive increase in the number of people who signed up for library cards in North Carolina. Annually, more than two hundred libraries in the state signed up for the program each year. Sixty-seven percent reported an increase in registration.

The state library used a Library Services and Technology Act grant to develop its public awareness efforts; more than sixty-five public library systems, representing 210 libraries, participated. The state library provided a range of resources to help member libraries get the word out about the Smartest Card; libraries could also order "Smartest Card" bags, bookmarks, and door hangers to distribute locally.

The North Carolina governor issued a proclamation in support of the campaign. Local officials endorsed it, visited their libraries, signed up for library cards, and read to children at story hour. Stories about the campaign ran in newspapers and on television and radio. Children across the state sported "Smartest Card" shoelaces. Renowned jazz musician Branford Marsalis served as its spokesperson in 2008. (Actress Andie McDowell was the spokesperson at the start of the effort.)

In Illinois, the Wauconda Area Library used the "Smartest Card" theme to attract more than five hundred new patrons. Hundreds more received replacement cards or keychain cards. More than 110 businesses offered discounts or freebies when their customers presented Wauconda Area Library cards during the promotion, and drawings were held for prizes that were donated by participating businesses.

In Michigan, staff of the Canton Public Library and the neighboring Plymouth District Library visited public and private schools with library card applications. Students received a "Smartest Card" library card wallet with their library card. With every visit to either library, they had their card stamped, and after four visits they received a prize. Approximately twelve hundred library cards were issued during the sign-up, and circulation in children's materials increased approximately 12 percent.

The Prairie Area Library System (PALS) in Illinois—with 376 member libraries of all types—promoted library services with the "Smartest Card" message. PALS ran ads in local movie theaters and an eight-page insert in fifty-eight local newspapers. Fliers, bookmarks, and other customizable print promotional materials were also made available to download from the PALS website, and libraries in the system could order various promotional products.

By the way, national polls conducted on behalf of ALA's Campaign for America's Libraries indicate an ongoing increase in the number of Americans who have library cards. The polls report more than two-thirds of all Americas say they have a library card, and the number is growing.

School Libraries: New Partnerships

In 2003, the American Association of School Librarians (AASL) developed the "@ your library Toolkit for School Library Media Programs." Even beyond the value of the individual tools and resources, the toolkit symbolizes the importance of promoting the school library media center and the role school library media specialists and good school library media programs play in student achievement.

The Minoa (New York) Elementary School library partnered with several local businesses and municipal agencies to promote reading and libraries during National Library Week 2007 and 2008. At a kick-off ceremony, the library presented partners with signs to display outside on the front doors of their buildings; each included customized slogans such as "Our Money Is on Reading" (at the local bank) and "You have the right to read" (at the police station). Each partner also received brochures about literacy and reading to distribute at its location. "The most exciting part of the project was the partnerships that surfaced because of the project," said Sue Kowalski, former Minoa Elementary School librarian. "Businesses we had never teamed up with are no longer strangers."

INFOhio, a statewide virtual information network for Ohio schools, used elements from the "@ your library Toolkit for School Library Media Programs" in its own guide, "Promoting INFOhio Resources to Parents." The guide was distributed to all Ohio K–12 school librarians to help them market INFOhio resources to parents.

Academic Libraries: Reaching Out to Students

Academic libraries were among the first to use the @ your library brand and Campaign for America's Libraries tools. In 2003, the Association for College and Research Libraries (ACRL), in conjunction with the campaign, introduced the "@ your library Toolkit for Academic and Research Libraries," which was designed to help libraries build local public awareness campaigns.

In 2004, American University Library used the toolkit and engaged university personnel and students to help implement an award-winning public awareness program to reach undergraduates. The library designed a campaign to raise awareness of the library's resources and build goodwill with students, centered around the themes "Are You in the Know?" and "Ask @ your library." The strategy was to create consistency and repetition of key messages through a welcome kit, a poster series, and media exposure. The library also worked with the campus marketing office and students in a marketing course in the School of Communication. The efforts paid off: the library was able to inform students about major building improvements and increase awareness of all of the library's resources, and in 2005 it won an ACRL best practices award.

Another award-winning campaign was created by the Milner Library at Illinois State University in Bloomington. After a campus survey in 2000 showed that many faculty and students did not know what library services were available, administrators created a permanent public relations position to increase aware-

ness. The @ your library brand was tied into key messages about the library and its goals, and "Ask a librarian @ your library" became the library's main message. New students received "Ask a librarian @ your library" pencils and Post-it notes at their first library tour, and the message appeared in daily activity calendars and in the campus newspaper. The @ your library brand was used in a number of other promotions, including a fund-raising campaign that raised about $2.3 million for the library.

"Having the ALA @ your library initiative provided the foundation on which to create key statements that carry out the library's message," said Toni Tucker, assistant to the dean for Public Relations and Outreach.

McMaster University, in Hamilton, Ontario, Canada, connected the @ your library brand to athletics and award-winning teachers to promote libraries. A poster campaign paired student athletes with taglines like "Tackle assignments @ your library" and "Hit the books @ your library." Another poster series linked the campaign back to teaching and learning at the library by featuring teaching award recipients and slogans such as "Revolutionary ideas @ your library." The library received the gold award in the Best Print Ad or Ad Campaign category of the annual Prix D'Excellence from the Canadian Council of Advancement of Education (CCAE).

Statewide Organizations

Library organizations such as ALA chapters, affiliates, and state libraries have used the @ your library brand to promote both campaign programs and their own initiatives:

In 2006, the Montana State Library promoted its Institute of Museum and Library Services–funded scholarship program with the theme, "A great career @ your library." Ten $25,000 scholarships were made available to Montana residents to earn an MLS through a correspondence course with the University of Washington.

The Colorado State Library hosted a bookmark design contest in 2006 with the theme, "Everyone is special @ your library." Three sets of bookmarks were created with the prize-winning art and were made available for download by all libraries in the state.

"See what's bubbling @ your library" was the 2008 summer reading theme in New Brunswick, Canada, sponsored by the New Brunswick Public Library Service. Sixty-one libraries and four bookmobiles in the province offered the summer reading program, with the theme focusing on science.

A Growing Resource for Local Libraries

Resources continue to be added to the @ your library website. Check out the website at www.ala.org/@your library/ for these great resources and more:

Download the @ your library brand in twenty-seven different languages.

For those outside urban areas, the "Small But Powerful Guide to Winning Big Support for Your Rural Library" online toolkit will walk you through how to develop your message and other key communication strategies.

Designed by children's librarians for children's librarians, the "Kids! @ your library" campaign was developed to help libraries reach out to kids and their parents and caregivers. The toolkit includes downloadable logos and an @ your library song developed specifically for the campaign, promotion tips, and sample press materials.

The "Speaking Up for Library Services to Teens: A Guide to Advocacy" toolkit includes resources for helping young-adult librarians make the case for the services they provide.

Why do we need libraries when we have the Internet? See "Tough Questions and Answers," also available on the @ your library website.

Sample press materials for promoting National Library Week and Library Card Sign-up Month are made available every year and can be customized for local media and for use in newsletters and websites.

Thousands of libraries of all types are connected to the Campaign for America's Libraries through the @ your library brand. They continue to participate in national promotions and develop their own creative initiatives to reach key audiences in their community. By using the brand, these communication efforts help create a more powerful and unified voice that highlights the value of libraries and librarians.

Kentucky Puts ALA Resources to Good Use

By Judith Gibbons

As resources from the American Library Association's Campaign for America's Libraries became available, so did the ways that Kentucky public libraries used these tools. At first, it was more passive participation, such as the occasional distribution of materials. For example, the Kentucky Department for Libraries and Archives (KDLA) bought items such as National Library Week materials annually and shipped them to public libraries statewide.

But ALA's Campaign for America's Libraries gave local practitioners the confidence to try novel ways to market services to the community. In Kentucky, as in many states, the number of true marketing professionals working in public libraries could be counted on the fingers of one hand. Library workers used ALA press materials and other collateral as the basis for library columns. ALA-generated proclamations were used locally and statewide. Tips for expanding library service would sometimes transition into new ways of providing services.

Sections of KDLA @ your library focused on the five values that the focus groups considered intrinsic to Kentucky's public libraries' basic values: democracy, lifelong learning, neighborliness, technology, and pride.

The KDLA's five-year plan (2003–2007) stated that the staff should "plan and execute a statewide communication and public awareness training program to assist and support librarians in raising awareness and marketing of their library and services and to increase the leadership role they have in the community." The focus was on practical learning, and the overarching theme was developing basic and usable public relations methods for Kentucky's public libraries.

Former KDLA colleague Kelly Reed summed up the program's success: "The participants . . . increased their skills in positioning themselves as community leaders and became more skilled in energizing their public libraries—and their partnerships with decision-makers in their counties."

Following another ALA lead, the Kentucky Public Library Association created a series of READ posters featuring legislators, state officials, librarians, and some prominent Kentuckians, including author Sue Grafton. The association used these during the 2008 legislative session as part of its efforts to secure more funds for public libraries, hanging them in the long tunnel that connects the Kentucky capitol building with legislative offices—prime space in which to share messages with state "movers and shakers." For two weeks, the association displayed the READ posters there, coupled with snapshots and quotes concerning the varied activities, programs, and people in the state's public libraries.

Every year, KDLA staff member Jay Bank has fun putting together "Quotable Facts about Kentucky's Libraries." Based on ALA's "Quotable Facts," this is a creative way to showcase local facts in a fashion tailored to the state or library service area. Here are three examples from 2007:

- If the 8,601,945 books in Kentucky public libraries were placed side by side, they would cover the entire length of Mammoth Cave, the world's largest cave system, at 365 miles.

- The number of KFC restaurants worldwide (more than 11,000) approximates the number of groups using meeting rooms in Kentucky's public libraries (12,552).

- More than 120,000 mint juleps were served at the 2007 Kentucky Derby, about one for each hour of bookmobile service in Kentucky during the past fiscal year.

In these ways and others, Kentuckians have localized ALA campaigns to win support and show the value of local public libraries. It has been a positive growth experience, putting theory into practice and demonstrating that, in Kentucky as elsewhere, the heart of the community is @ your library.

Judith Gibbons was director of field services for the Kentucky Department of Libraries and Archives and chair of the ALA Public Awareness Committee. She retired in 2008.

9

AMPLIFY YOUR MESSAGES THROUGH PARTNERSHIPS TO REACH BROADER AUDIENCES

Megan Humphrey

Partnerships can have enormous impact on your public awareness efforts. When ALA launched the popular Campaign for America's Libraries, the public awareness campaign that highlights the value of libraries and librarians and involves thousands of libraries of all types, partnerships were considered to be a way "to help broaden the scope and reach of the campaign." That turned out to be an understatement.

Partnerships with national organizations have impressively extended the reach of campaign messages. The cumulative effect has brought a renewed energy to the promotion of libraries and librarians and helped make the @ your library brand part of the language of libraries. And partnerships have returned more than a $13 to $1 return on investment.

Partnerships in your community can extend the reach of your organization well beyond the traditional library audience. Partnering with corporations or other organizations can provide the resources you need to reach out to a broad audience or a targeted one. They also can give you access to powerful communication channels including your partners' advertising, media relations efforts, website, or though such promotional tools as contests, giveaways, and more.

The Initiatives and Projects section of the Campaign for America's Libraries website (www.ala.org/@yourlibrary/), provides library success stories from all types of libraries that have developed such partnerships; many of these examples can be adapted by your library.

Here are some examples intended to inspire communicators to think creatively about possible collaborations—and about the resources available through ALA that will help you reach the library community and beyond with your messages.

Two American Institutions: Libraries and Baseball

Baseball is a great vehicle to reach library supporters and baseball fans. In 2001 "Join the Major Leagues @ your library," a partnership between the Campaign for America's

Libraries and Major League Baseball, was designed to promote computer literacy. Participants were invited to participate in an online baseball trivia contest that was open to all ages. They were encouraged to use the print and electronic resources at their library to look up the answers to the trivia questions. One person who answered all of the questions correctly was selected as the winner of a trip to the World Series.

ALA developed the program's website and a toolkit—sample press releases, program ideas, and a logo that could be used on local publicity materials—to help libraries promote the program. Major league baseball players participated in events in libraries, and their appearances enjoyed extensive media coverage.

The program evolved into "Step Up to the Plate @ your library," a current partnership between the National Baseball Hall of Fame and Museum and the Campaign for America's Libraries. Local libraries brought the program home in many creative ways. You can engage your local professional team—whether it is a major or minor league team. Here are some examples of what libraries are doing:

The Philadelphia Force, a professional women's softball team, helped the Avon Grove Library of West Grove, Pennsylvania, promote "Step Up to the Plate." Force players read stories, made baseball-themed crafts, and autographed pink softballs.

The Newport News (Virginia) Public Library System created its own Step Up to the Plate @ your library summer reading program. All age groups were encouraged to participate, and adult readers were entered in drawings for weekly prizes from the Norfolk Tides, a local minor league team.

The Hockessin (Delaware) Public Library hosted a baseball day that included the reading of a pop-up version of *Take Me Out to the Ball Game* and baseball-themed crafts and movies. Each child who turned in a Step Up to the Plate playbook received a pack of playing cards donated by the Roberto Clemente Foundation; other prizes included tickets to a Philadelphia Phillies game, donated by a Friends group.

Visit the website at www.ala.org/baseball/ for more information.

National Magazine, Local Impact

The Campaign for America's Libraries partnership with *Woman's Day* magazine began as a program called "Put It in Writing @ your library." It was designed to promote the wealth of opportunities that libraries offer aspiring writers. From 2002 to 2006, fifty-four public and community college libraries hosted writing workshops that were led by writers from the magazine. *Woman's Day* publicized the workshops in its March issue each year. Nearly four thousand people nationwide attended.

Woman's Day (www.womansday.com) currently partners with ALA on a contest that encourages its four million readers to contribute their thoughts on a library-related topic each year. This promotion generates extensive publicity and can serve as a model for a local library and a community-based media outlet partnership.

For example, the 2007 initiative asked readers to describe why they love their library. The response was overwhelming. More than three thousand people sent in personal stories, the biggest response to any *Woman's Day* promotion of this nature. The four best stories were published in the magazine. In 2009, the magazine will publish the winners of a contest that asked readers to describe how they have used the library to improve their health. The next promotion will ask "How can libraries help patrons during economic hard times?"

Your library can promote these initiatives. Check the campaign website, www.ala.org/@yourlibrary/, for more details.

Targeted PSAs: "Yo te puedo ayudar"

ALA members identified Hispanics/Latinos as an important audience for targeted outreach. A survey by ALA indicated that fewer than half (49 percent) of this rapidly growing subpopulation used their libraries in 2006, compared with 63 percent of whites and 64 percent of African Americans.

ALA's Campaign for America's Libraries partnered with Univision Radio, the largest Spanish language radio network, to launch a public service announcement (PSA) campaign targeting Hispanic/Latino populations. Focusing on interpersonal relationships and building trust, the campaign presents the librarian as a provider of information and support, capable of opening up the wide range of opportunities represented by the local library—books and information about health, getting a job, and starting a business, among other things. The primary message is "Yo te puedo ayudar" ("I can help you"). Some of the PSAs star Univision Radio personality Javier Romero.

Univision began airing the PSAs in nine major metropolitan markets and promoted use of the PSAs across its network of seventy stations. The library messages in the PSAs reached 50 percent of the U.S. Spanish-speaking population. The program also has a Spanish language website (www.entubiblioteca.org) that supports the messages of the campaign.

And as usual, ALA created tools, including bookmarks, an ad, a poster, and web buttons, that libraries can download and use locally.

Grant Opportunities

Foundations are great partners. "The American Dream Starts @ your library," for example, is a partnership with the Dollar General discount retailer that reinforces the vital role that public libraries play in reaching out to adult English speakers—and is funded through a grant from the Dollar General Literacy Foundation. In April 2008, the initiative awarded funding to thirty-four public libraries in nineteen states to add or expand literacy services for adult English-language learners, and an accompanying online toolkit (www.americandreamtoolkit.org) provides resources, service models, and examples of best practices collected from local libraries. The program is administered by ALA's Office for Literacy and Outreach Services.

Carnegie Corporation of New York has awarded the American Library Association a grant to support the Carnegie Corporation of New York/*New York Times* I Love My Librarian Award.

The award launched in 2008 and will continue through 2013. It encourages library users to recognize the accomplishments of librarians for their efforts to improve the lives of people in their community. More than thirty-two hundred nominations were received in 2008.

Up to ten librarians in public, school, and academic libraries will be selected each year and honored at a ceremony and reception at The TimesCenter, hosted by the *New York Times*. Each partner receives a $5,000 cash award, a plaque, and a travel stipend to attend the awards reception.

For more information, visit www.ilovelibraries.org/ilovemylibrarian/.

Partnership Tips

Here are tips on how to form effective partnerships:

- Start with who you know. Who are your allies? Which groups might you already be aligned with? Would a formal partnership help further their goals—and yours?
- Identify your goals. Look for groups that have similar interests and values that might be able to offer additional resources and reach.
- Identify what you have to offer. What are the strengths of your library or organization that would be of value to other groups?
- Explore what prospective partners have to offer. Can they help you amplify your messages?
- Take the time to develop a relationship. Educate prospective partners so they have a clear understanding of the value of libraries and their impact on the community.
- Before entering a partnership, be clear about what both sides will offer.
- Seek maximum visibility for partnerships. Use your mutual project as an opportunity to gain ongoing attention for your library.

Partnerships offer libraries a wonderful opportunity to obtain more resources for their public awareness efforts—helping reach broader and more targeted audiences as well.

10

AFFORDABLE PODCASTS FOR LIBRARIES

Steve Zalusky

With the communication universe expanding, libraries are using new tools to inform library patrons and the world at large about the great resources they offer. One of the tools enjoying increasing—and effective—use is podcasting.

Communicators are finding that the mobility of podcasts has great appeal and makes their message more engaging; you can download a podcast to an iPod or other mobile media device and listen to it while traveling or even multitasking. As society grows more mobile, delivering information to an audience on the go, whether traveling by car or train or even jogging, becomes more of a necessity.

Podcasts also offer the advantage of spreading the message through the human voice or image, rather than the dry medium of the printed page.

Pod People

The podcasting universe is a vast terrain; you can find audio podcasts from such media giants as NPR and ESPN, as well as video podcasts from MTV and CBS.

Libraries and library associations are also boarding the podcasting bandwagon. "Games in Libraries" is a monthly podcast that bills itself as for "librarians interested in learning more about games, gamers, and gaming that might be appropriate for use in their library services." The podcast's producer, Scott Nicholson, also produces a video podcast about games called "Board Games with Scott."

Nicholson, program director for the library and information science program at the Syracuse University School of Information Studies, said, "What I wanted to do with my video podcast was teach people how to play games, and I knew a video demonstration would be much more effective than simply an audio description of the game component. The 'Games in Libraries' audio podcast is about building a community of librarians interested in gaming, bringing the same type of discussions typically had at conferences to any librarian with an MP3 player."

David Free, editor in chief of *College and Research Libraries News* and marketing/communications specialist with the Association of College and Research Libraries, a division of ALA, is an innovator in library podcasting. Free started podcasting in early 2005 when he was a public services librarian at the Decatur Campus Library of Georgia Perimeter College. He had run across the concept from a library blogger named Greg Schwartz.

Pam Jaskot, consultant to the State Library of North Carolina, produces podcasts for the web page of the state's Department of Cultural Resources—the state library is a branch of the department. As part of the ALA's "Smartest Card @ your library" campaign, Jaskot hosted a podcast featuring world-renowned saxophonist Branford Marsalis. Marsalis, spokesperson for the state library's "Smartest Card" campaign, urged North Carolina residents to visit their local library to get the smartest card—a library card. He also related his experiences with libraries during his formative years.

Do-It-Yourself Podcasts

So how can you, the librarian, take the plunge into the podcasting pool? It's really simple.

The easiest way to start is by setting up a blog, which is basically a journal published on the Internet. Free blogging sites are available at such sites as www.blogger.com and www.wordpress.com.

Viewers can subscribe to your blog and download your podcasts through what is known as an RSS feed. RSS stands for Really Simple Syndication. It is a way for people to track information in one place from multiple sources on the Internet through an RSS "reader." One example is Google Reader; other readers include Newsgator and Bloglines. The reader lets you subscribe to various websites and blogs. Once you subscribe, you don't even have to look for articles and blog posts; they look for you.

"Having a blog, as opposed to a website, does kind of make it easier for the RSS feed part. That's an integral part of podcasting," said Free. "It gets the content out to people without them having to come to you to see whether there are going to be new episodes posted."

Audio Recording and Editing

Once you've set up your blog, you have to consider what kind of recording and editing equipment to choose for your podcast. Choosing the right equipment will be one of your most important decisions, especially when selecting the proper recording devices.

When selecting a microphone for audio podcasts, your options run the gamut from inexpensive USB microphones to CD-quality USB microphones (that plug into your computer's USB port), which cost in the $100-to-$200 range.

"If I'm doing an in-person studio recording, I use a studio-quality USB mic and a laptop," Free said, adding that he records conference calls using a voice-over IP system called Skype. He said there is a plug-in called Power Grammo that lets you record Skype phone calls. Free said a Skype pro account is very inexpensive for one year.

Free said another USB mic you can use is the Snowball, manufactured by Blue Microphones and sold for around $140, although you can get deals on Amazon.com. Nicholson said you can start out with an inexpensive USB headset microphone like the one manufactured by Plantronics for $40. "Plantronics headset mics are excellent quality," he said.

You can also use a Belkin microphone attached to an iPod. This can be an effective solution for on-location interviewing, when you can't necessarily carry around your computer and record on a USB mic.

Now that you have your equipment, it's time to consider where you'll record your podcast.

"You're going to need some kind of quiet location," Free said. An office that is isolated and devoid of background noise will suffice. "You don't need to create your own recording studio in your library, although certainly if you have resources to do that, that would be awesome. Depending on how loud your HVAC is, if you have control over it, turn it off. . . . Things like HVAC and other background noises are some things to consider."

Adding a Video Component

Blogging software also enables you to produce video podcasts. If you choose to shoot video, a number of affordable cameras are available, some for as little as $100 (such as the Flip camcorder). Here are some tips for recording video:

- Visual elements that need to be considered include lighting, wardrobe, positioning and movement of the camera, and even special effects.
- You need to take care in editing. Editing video can be difficult, since taking out dead air or the occasional *uhh* or *umm* can also lead to jumpiness in the visual. Those can be bridged over by inserting stills or dissolves.
- Editing can also be expensive, depending on whether you want to use a program like the Mac's iMovie that already comes with the computer, or move to another level with a program called Final Cut Pro, which can cost in the $500 range.

Nicholson said that built-in tools like iMovie or Windows Movie Maker are great places to start making videos; his first ten videos were done in iMovie. "These free tools are designed to be as easy as possible in helping you take a single stream of footage, edit it a little bit, and put it online," he said.

As a library gains experience and wants to do more sophisticated things like layering multiple video and audio streams, these free tools will not work as well.

Nicholson added, "You'll know when it's time to look for more advanced software when you can't figure out how to do something in the basic tools—the capabilities just aren't in those programs."

Nicholson uses Final Cut Express on the Mac and Adobe Premiere on the PC.

Tips on Editing Software

Good editing software is also important. For audio podcasts, both Free and Nicholson recommend Audacity, which can be used with both Mac and PC systems and is available for free online at http://audacity.source forge.net. Audacity has the additional advantage that you can record as well as edit with it.

Nicholson also recommended Amadeus Pro—a multitrack editor that HairerSoft sells for around $40—to record and edit the actual files. He said he then takes the individual files and mixes the sound in GarageBand, a program that comes with Macintosh computers. At this point, he has not saved his project as an MP3 file. "As soon as you compress it into the MP3, the file loses quality, but you reduce the file size by 90 percent."

Nicholson said he uses a free program called the Levelator (http://the-levelator.en.softonic.com) to equalize the sound levels.

The final step, Nicholson said, is converting the project to an MP3 file in Audacity, iTunes, or any other audio tool that can do the compression.

Taking It to Another Level

If you become proficient enough with video, or if you feel limited by your existing equipment, you might want to invest in something more professional.

Randy McComas and Bob Belinoff of Digital Workshop, based in Albuquerque, New Mexico, produced the video shown at the 2008 ALA Annual Conference Opening General Session. McComas said he and Belinoff use the smaller digital cameras, what are known as "prosumer" cameras (professional consumer). "It's got the bells and whistles and features that I would need as a professional, but the camera is smaller and can be operated by consumers," he said.

But McComas warns that his camera costs as much as $5,000. "The one we have is a Panasonic AG-DVX100B. The price is coming down and the reason is because it's standard-definition. With the world going toward high-definition, those cameras are going to continue to get cheaper. For blogs and podcasts, they would be great . . ."

He recommends a prosumer camera with a flip-out LCD screen for under $1,000, probably a Sony or a Panasonic.

Going Live

Once you've produced your podcast, it is a simple matter to attach the file to your blog or a site that provides RSS feeds. Most blogging software now has a plug-in or some form of built-in support for podcasting. WordPress, for example, has a plug-in called PodPress.

One way to start an RSS feed is by storing your video or audio file on a web hosting service like LibSyn (short for "liberated syndication"), which is available to subscribers for as little as $5 or $10 per month. According to the LibSyn website, "Liberated Syndication goes beyond traditional webhosting—we are syndication providers. You get a home to store your media, a simple but powerful blog engine, an RSS feed, and an interface to distribute your podcast to a limitless audience. Our service also works with your existing blog." But that is only one of many options; another site that is completely free is blip.tv, which allows you to upload either audio or video files and provides an RSS feed for them. Once the file is uploaded, you can also copy some code into your blog to make the file available for listening or viewing on your website.

In addition, an excellent place to park your podcast is the Internet Archive (www.archive.org). The Internet Archive allows you to post large files at no cost. Users have stored everything from Grateful Dead concerts to old radio shows and newsreels.

And Now Back to You

As you can see, you can absorb in a very short time what you need to learn to podcast effectively, at relatively little cost for initial capital outlay and with virtually no ongoing costs.

More important, podcasting means you are in control of getting your message out in a way that is easily accessible to others. With the advent of social networking sites like Facebook and MySpace, this message is infinitely sharable, since sites like MySpace allow you to upload video and then post it to your MySpace blog.

Additional Resources on Podcasting

Find more on podcasting on these sites:

www.libsuccess.org/index.php?title=Podcasting
http://podcasting101.pbwiki.com
www.slideshare.net/search/slideshow?q=podcasting+libraries&x=0&y=0
www.wo.ala.org/districtdispatch/?p=197
www.infotoday.com/cilmag/apr06/Eash.shtml
http://lis757.blogwithoutalibrary.net/2006/?p=62
www.oregonlibraries.net/staff/wiki/IL05Podcasts
http://wikis.ala.org/yalsa/index.php/Teens_Podcasting_@_Your_Library:_A_Getting_
     Started_Guide
http://speakfreelywithpodcasts.wikispaces.com/Podcasting+Resources

11

GAMING @ YOUR LIBRARY
Generate Excitement in Social Settings to Increase Attendance at Your Library

Dale Lipschultz

EDITOR'S NOTE

Communicators in libraries around the country have noticed a sizable increase in interest in gaming at libraries both by patrons and the news media.

To publicize the trend of gaming in libraries, the American Library Association's first ever National Gaming Day was held Saturday, November 15, 2008. On that day, more than fourteen thousand people of all ages participated in gaming activities at more than six hundred libraries around the country.

An estimated fifty-five hundred library patrons joined the ALA in establishing the record for the highest number of people playing the same board game on the same day at the library. More than sixteen thousand public, school, and academic libraries received a copy of Pictureka!, a frenzied version of finders keepers that was donated by Hasbro for use during National Gaming Day.

Role-playing games were also very popular during National Gaming Day. Registered libraries reported that more than eleven hundred library gamers played Dungeons and Dragons role-playing game as well as Magic: The Gathering trading-card game (donated by Wizards of the Coast).

A list of gaming blogs that communicators may find useful as they develop their promotional efforts on behalf of gaming activity at their library can be found in the appendix to this chapter.

Communicators have witnessed a dramatic growth in gaming activities in libraries of all kinds. They have also seen library patrons of all ages participate; today, age no longer corresponds to interest, aptitude, or expertise in gaming. What matters is the opportunity for play, a willingness to learn, the supportive presence of experts and novices, and the library as the setting for learning, playing, and gaming.

Infants and toddlers learn about the world through the people they interact with and the games they play. Toddlers play independently, parallel to their peers, and with their caregivers. They experiment with objects, movement, and language both verbal and in print. Preschool children love playing traditional board games like Candyland and Chutes and Ladders and through play, learn to take turns and cooperate while developing early literacy skills.

For children in school, their school library and media center can be the epicenter for work and play. School librarians use modern board games to provide rich game environments with strong content connections and with plenty of fun; they also select certain video games to encourage teamwork and help develop critical thinking skills.

Finally, twenty-first-century gaming is not just for kids. The older adults at the Old Bridge (New Jersey) Public Library Senior Spaces learned all about the Wii from specially trained teen mentors. In the context of this social and slightly competitive activity, teens became teachers, seniors became learners and gamers, and everybody won!

Here are some gaming case studies that target key audiences and can build excitement and attendance at your library. Use these examples to help create your own programs.

Preschoolers Love Games and "Great Games! Family Day"

"Every Child Ready to Read @ your library" is a joint project of the ALA's Public Library Association and the Association for Library Service to Children. This initiative has helped caregivers appreciate the importance of modeling word play during library story times. Rhyming, listening, and letter recognition games promote early language and literacy development. In addition, memory and matching board and computer games help preschoolers move from spoken language to print.

In April 2007, the Allen County Public Library in Fort Wayne, Indiana, held "Great Games! Family Day." The event included board and video games for all ages. Teresa Wall, children's librarian, helped a group of preschoolers play familiar and new board games. Wall said that the young children enjoyed experimenting with board games designed for older children. They invented their own rules and used game pieces and pictures to create new, nontext scenarios. She also noted that many of the preschoolers wanted to use the Wii. She was pleased to see that while waiting and playing, young children were patient, polite, and helpful to each other.

Wall knows that many tech-savvy, twenty-first-century caregivers are eager to share computer games with their infants and toddlers. She's observed babies as young as six months playing Giggles Computer Funtime on the computer while sitting in their caregivers' laps. Each time a key is struck, the screen image changes to display colors, shapes, and familiar images, to the child's delight.

Work and Play at the School Library

Most librarians grew up being told to finish their work before they played. Now libraries across the country are encouraging children to get busy with their play. Games in modern school, public, and academic libraries offer a learning environment that is compatible with fun. This is not a new idea, but a new focus on different types of games has revealed the potential for the medium as part of your library collections and programs.

The School Library System of Genesee Valley Board of Cooperative Educational Services, part of a New York State educational service agency providing support to twenty-two rural districts in the western part of the state, started a game library in 2007 to provide curriculum-aligned instructional resources to member libraries. Working from the new *Standards for the 21st-Century Learner* published by the American Association of School Librarians, Christopher Harris and Brian Mayer selected games that teach students about inquiry, use of information resources, participation in knowledge-based collaborations, and other critical thinking skills.

What has made the program so successful is a dedication to using authentic games with a high level of play value that also happen to be aligned with library and state content curriculum standards. Students can see right through so-called *educational games* that have been developed to teach, but modern board games provide rich game environments with strong content connections along with plenty of fun. A game like 1960: The Making of the President, though not developed for schools or intended as an instructional resource, immerses students in the famous Nixon-Kennedy election using cards with primary source pictures and descriptions of historical events to enrich learning.

Using games to support learning is not a new idea; in fact, one might easily suggest that it is perhaps an instinctual impulse that we have been mistakenly repressing for too long. Young animals, for instance, learn the skills to survive through mock hunting of their siblings or parents. Small children also learn to emulate productive adult behaviors through role-playing and interaction with toys. With the emergence of video games, educators discovered a more immersive environment that can provide a more detailed simulation of reality.

As Dr. James Paul Gee, an education professor at the University of Wisconsin—Madison explored in *What Video Games Have to Teach Us about Learning and Literacy*, these games provide a safe environment where students can explore and learn.[1] Some computer and video games like the Civilization or Age of Empires series are commercial successes that have strong teaching and learning connections. More recently, so-called serious games like the United Nation's Food Force have been designed with a specific instructional purpose.

At the Keller Global Science Middle School in Clark County, Nevada, librarian Karen Egger is using a Nintendo Wii and computer games as part of an after-school program for students. This self-described "non–techno geek" offers a simple explanation for her use of these new technologies: "I selected these particular games to encourage teamwork and critical thinking skills." Whether in a school, public, or academic library, games can support our shared mission of helping our patrons become more informed participants in an information-based society.

Gaming with Older Adults and Teens

"The Old Bridge Public Library began gaming with teens more than four years ago," says Allan Kleiman, Senior Spaces manager. "In 2007, we saw gaming take off with older adults in senior centers and nursing homes. Seniors everywhere were using the Wii to bowl, play tennis, and box! Why not libraries?"

Teen librarian Theresa Wordelman and Kleiman developed plans for the first older adults gaming day with teens as mentors and training instructors. First, the teens went through a screening and training process. They needed to be able to teach Wordelman and Kleiman to use the Wii. Those selected for the gaming event were given basic instructions on how older adults learn, problem solving, and most important, how to instill confidence in these novice players regardless of their age. Wordelman and Kleiman report:

Initially, we wanted to introduce older adults to twenty-first-century gaming and encourage them to play. To accomplish this we set up three areas in the library's meeting room. Area one was Wii bowling projected on a big screen, area two was Guitar Hero II, and area three was Big Brain Academy.

Each older adult was assigned a teen mentor. Teens were genuinely excited to demonstrate the games and the older adults were very pleased to have their own teen mentor. Within fifteen minutes the room was rocking. Music was playing, bowling pins were crashing, and Brain Age Academy was beeping. There were surprises all around. The teens were surprised by the older adults' curiosity and the older adults were impressed by the teens teaching skills. This event was a win-win for all.

For several months, the teen mentors continued to work with the older adults at Senior Spaces gaming events. It wasn't long until the older adults became accomplished gamers and confident teachers. As for the teens, they continued to have a role in Senior Spaces. "Our teens introduced their parents and grandparents to gaming at the library and they returned to play and compete with the older adults they once mentored. In fact, the teen-mentors and older adults held a reunion in mid-December 2008. The activity—an intergenerational Wii Bowling Tournament," said Wordelman and Kleiman.

The gaming in Senior Spaces has been the catalyst for developing gaming activities for children, tweens, and teens at the Central Library and the Laurence Harbor Branch. "We've tried everything from a Halo 2 tournament to Super Mario Brothers Kart. We've also had open gaming using our in-library collection of Wii games. We've purchased game tie-in books to help players improve their skills," said Wordelman and Kleiman. "In addition, all library staff has been introduced to gaming at our library's annual staff day. We've achieved buy-in from staff at all levels. They now understand and appreciate just why playing games at the library is so popular with our customers—regardless of age."

In each case history, the games and players changed. In spite of these differences, strong themes ran through all of the gaming activities. Play, from infancy to old age, is an essential part of living and learning. Play at the library is a profoundly social activity that brings together experts and novices, seniors and children. Finally, the gaming experience matters as much, or more than, the game—who you play with, who you learn from, and finally, where you play. Playing games in the library is a great way for communicators to promote learning and attendance. Let the games begin!

APPENDIX
A Selected List of Gaming Blogs

1up (www.1up.com): Updates multiple times a day. Written by game designers and other industry professionals for the general public.

The Escapist (www.escapistmagazine.com): Updates weekly. Written for gamers by gamers and amateur journalists.

Gamasutra (www.gamasutra.com): Updates multiple times a day. Written for game developers.

GamePolitics (www.gamepolitics.com): Updates multiple times a day. Written for anyone interested in the crossover between politics and video games. Hosted by the Entertainment Consumers' Association.

Gamer Dad (www.gamingwithchildren.com): Updates almost daily. Written for parents and caregivers.

Gaming in Libraries (http://gaming.ala.org/news/): Updates semi-regularly. Written for librarians who offer or are considering providing gaming to patrons of all ages.

ICv2 (http://icv2.com): Updates multiple times a day. Written for librarians and businesses.

Joystiq (www.joystiq.com): Updates multiple times a day. Written for average gamers to cut through the hype and offer a unique focus on gamer culture.

Kotaku (http://kotaku.com): Updates multiple times a day. Written for gamers from all over the world.

Library Gamer (http://librarygamer.word press.com): Updates a few times each month. Written primarily for school media specialists.

Ypulse (www.ypulse.com): Updates daily. Written for media and marketing professionals.

NOTE

1. James Paul Gee, *What Video Games Have to Teach Us about Learning and Literacy* (New York: Palgrave Macmillan, 2003).

12

A VALUES-BASED APPROACH TO SUCCESSFUL LIBRARY ADVOCACY

Laura K. Lee Dellinger

In communities throughout the United States today, change is the buzzword. The face of America has become many faces, reflecting our increasing cultural and ethnic diversity and simultaneously highlighting—in the wake of a historic presidential election—common values shared by all Americans such as opportunity, education, fairness, access, and family. And while it can be argued that there have never been wider gaps between those who have and those who don't, those who succeed in school and those who don't, those who can afford homes or health care and those who can't, there has not been a time in modern memory where the need to address these gaps has been more a part of the public discourse. It is against this backdrop that the American library shines as an example of a vehicle that can serve to level the playing field.

Today's libraries face ongoing challenges: funding shortages and lack of clarity about their resources, role, and value (often as people remember libraries to be, not as how they function today). These and other challenges are real and urgent, and they call for solutions based on our shared values. The need for you as a library leader to play an increased role in advocating for your library (and by extension for the potential and opportunity that exists in every community) has never been greater. And make no mistake about it—advocacy is indeed your role. You do it every time you highlight how a reading program creates building blocks for a lifetime of literacy skills; or showcase the value of online resources to job hunters who seek a better life for their families; or invite the community into your facility to hear a lecture from an author whose latest work tells the story of respect and tolerance in a multicultural world. Your library connects with your customers every day based on what they need and what is most valuable and useful to them; in short, what aligns with their values. And your library advocacy efforts can and should do the same thing. This chapter highlights an approach to advocacy that is based in community values and builds upon other communication approaches commonly used by libraries. We'll examine first the broad communication approaches, then dig a bit deeper into what we mean by advocacy, and ultimately walk through a series of questions that serve as your guide to building effective advocacy plans yourself.

At the heart of the role of advocate lies communication, the ultimate purpose of which is always to gain a response from your audience. Clearly, audience response and action are core needs for libraries of all types and sizes in all locations. Gaining audiences' response requires that you are establishing true opportunities for communication that are two-way. This dynamic approach begins with listening to your communities'/stakeholders' needs and values, evaluating them, and then illustrating the ways your library delivers service that responds to what your constituency believes matters most. There are a variety of communication practices that are commonly used in libraries, each of which deserves attention. They include marketing, public relations, and advocacy. While each has a distinct purpose, all are approaches to telling the story of your library on an ongoing basis and increasing perceived value among library constituencies for your valuable resources, programs, and services. Remember, external audiences do not know or care which department or function generated the communication; they perceive it all as coming from the library, and their response will be to their aggregate experience.

While the focus in this chapter is advocacy, it's helpful to understand how advocacy is different from other efforts and what types of challenges are best addressed by each. This helps us see the ways in which a well-crafted communication program can combine communication approaches and more effectively ensure your library is connecting with the people who use, support, and fund you and enable you to build support for core issues that affect library services.

Let's turn first to marketing. Marketing is focused on creating a *transaction* between a customer and the provider of a service, program, or product. Marketing is best used by libraries to do some of the following:

- increase program participation
- increase the number of card holders
- reach special populations for programs
- engage specific audiences to use key services

Promotions are used to gain participation in upcoming events, bring people to hear a speaker, use a service, sign up for a program, check out a book, or take advantage of a specific library program, service, or resource.

Brochures, posters, fliers, e-mails, and other traditional tools are commonly used for marketing purposes.

Closely related to the marketing function is a practice known as public relations. Public relations efforts focus on creating mutually beneficial relationships between an organization and the audiences key to its success.

Public relations is best used by libraries to create and sustain long-term relationships with stakeholders, friends, funders, voters, community leaders, potential partners, media, and others whose influence and contributions are necessary. It supports marketing and advocacy efforts because it is focused on the long-term and enables you to build relationships with your media outlets, key community organizations, and other groups within your institutional structure (e.g., other departments, city/county work units, colleges, etc.). Stories in community, institutional and/or mass media outlets, partnerships developed to benefit your library, sponsorships that help further your goals, and many of the same tools used in marketing are also common tools in public relations.

The third leg of the communication stool is advocacy. A dictionary definition of advocate is "to support or urge by argument, especially publicly." In other words, advocacy is building a case for support for a cause and getting your audience to say "yes." Advocacy is best used by libraries to advance *specific* proposals such as funding or policy questions, and to advance specific issues (e.g., budget approval, bond or levy funding, early literacy, freedom of speech/press/information, privacy rights, publisher mergers, etc.). It is also a powerful tool for libraries to help advance causes beyond their specific institutional needs but relevant to the fulfillment of their mission (freedom of information, free speech, copyright law that balances private gain with public good, etc.).

The Advocacy Process at Work

Successful advocacy begins with asking questions. Before you start your advocacy work, it is vital that you inquire into what the real issues or problems are and explore the reasons why these issues/problems exist at the deeper social level, not just in your library. These are critical steps because they help you begin to frame your case in terms of the needs of your audience and explore solutions that help your library advance the broader social need. This approach will ensure that your advocacy is grounded in reasons that actually matter outside the walls of your library. This chapter is organized based on a series of questions that should guide all of your advocacy efforts. These questions are grouped into four categories: purpose, people, persuasion, and performance.

STEP 1.
Defining Your Purpose

At the start of your advocacy efforts, it's essential to step back and ask these formative questions:

- What is the problem or need we are trying to address?
- What is the cause?
- Why do you need to address this problem?
- How do you want to solve the problem/ meet the need?
- How will your solution address the broader needs?
- What is your goal?

The first step in defining your purpose is to get clarity about the problem or need itself. Often, advocacy efforts don't work because we have not *accurately* defined the problem or need and we aren't clear about how to address it or what we want others to do about it. Other times we have artificially limited the problem in a way that focuses on how the problem affects the library and not on the broader community/audience need that the library may be unable to meet unless the problem is solved.

Let's turn to the challenge faced by the fictional institution known as Libraryland. Here's what we know: Libraryland is funded from tax revenue and is a part of the budget of Cityville, a midsized community located about an hour from the largest metropolitan area in Anystate. Over the past ten years, Cityville has experienced substantial changes as a community. The population has increased by 50 percent; its economy, once focused in manufacturing and transportation, has become increasingly an information technology economy; and more than 25 percent of new residents have come from adjacent metropolitan areas with well-funded (and much larger) library systems, bringing with them more urban expectations than Cityville is currently able to meet. The popula-

tion is fairly split between long-time residents, most of whom have grown children who have long since left Cityville, and new residents, who are predominantly young families and include a significant number of Russian immigrants, along with a large and growing Latino population. Despite the population growth, the library has experienced a number of budget cuts over the last few years, resulting in shortened hours, limited purchasing of new materials and online resources, and increasingly outdated computer technology. Despite the economic challenges, the community continues to demand increased services and resources; however, the city government generally believes that the library is "doing fine" and plans to invest heavily in public safety (police and fire). The task for Libraryland is to advocate for restoration and then growth of the library's budget to meet the community's needs. A volunteer group called Libraries4Life has come together to support the library and wants to be a partner in Libraryland's efforts.

Applying our questions to the situation, let's look more closely at this scenario.

What is the problem or need? Libraryland recently conducted a needs assessment of Cityville residents to learn more about what they wanted from their library. Community members seek increased computer access, expanded access to books and materials, more support in the form of programs for young people, and adult learning opportunities including ESL classes. The demand is greater than the library's ability to meet it. (Note: The need is being defined here as the community's need, not the library's need.)

What is the cause? Changing demographics, an increasing population base, and stagnant funding to support library services. (Note: When assessing cause, be sure to look at what has or has not changed. Examples: population increase, loss of a major employer, expiring bond, and decreased general fund resources.)

Why do you need to address this problem? Community members seek opportunities to learn, expand their skill sets, ensure the education of their children, and bridge the digital divide that separates those who can afford computers and Internet access and those who cannot. The community is currently unhappy with the level of service being provided to them and wants more. Without addressing these community needs, Cityville will risk reversing its trend of attracting new community members and continuing to grow and diversify its economy. Residents have high expectations of Cityville, and unmet expectations translate into unhappy voters. (Note: You should frame the *why* in terms of the social impact vs. the library-centric impact of not enough money.)

How do you want to solve the problem or meet the need? The library proposes that to meet the community's needs, it would need to expand hours of operation to seven days a week, increase the number of computer terminals by 25 percent, add back ESL and early learning programs that were cut from the last budget, and grow the collection of books, materials, and relevant online databases to levels sufficient to meet expectations. (Note: The solution is *not* money; money is what pays for the solution. This distinction is important because when the argument becomes focused on money alone, your opportunity to build a persuasive case is diminished.)

How will your solution address the broader needs? This solution enables service delivery at a level the community demands, helps children start school ready to learn, helps adults learn new language skills, and helps bridge the technology gap experienced by a significant portion of the community.

What is your goal? To implement the solutions necessary to answer the community's needs, the library must convince Cityville to increase funding to Libraryland by 7 percent.

Armed with this understanding of your situation and the approach you seek to take to address it, you can begin to look at how to reach your goal. The next step is to understand who can help.

STEP 2.
People—Identifying and Understanding Your Audiences

The next step is defining and understanding what motivates your audience. There are two questions that must be answered in this step:

- Who are the people (audiences) who can help you make your goal a reality?
- What are their values, needs, and motivators? (What is important to them, not necessarily about the library, but more generally in their day-to-day lives?)

In order to achieve your advocacy goals, you must focus on the people who can help get you what you want. You probably already know many of the people or kinds of people who could help you successfully advocate for your issue. The illustration below shows some of the broad categories of audiences for libraries. It is important to think about your community and its specific social, economic, political, and cultural audiences. Remember, effective advocacy *must* be targeted; you can still serve your entire constituency, but you need to focus on getting key audience groups to take action for your advocacy efforts to be successful.

It is helpful to think of your audiences in two major categories: primary audiences and secondary audiences. Primary audiences are those people who can actually make the decision you are advocating. In our example, the elected officials on the Cityville City Council are the audience that will make the decision. Secondary audiences are those who influence the primary audience, and they are often the best messengers to help advocate for the solution you proposed. In the Cityville example, secondary audiences could include leaders of education and cultural institutions in the community, business leaders and employers, Realtors, community opinion leaders, and individuals who can speak firsthand about the importance of the resources Libraryland offers to them or their families. In many communities specific individual influencers would include large or consistent donors to city council members' campaigns as well as known advisors and/or appointees to commissions and committees. The knowledge of existing trusted relationships between secondary audiences and the primary decision makers can help increase the efficiency and impact of your advocacy efforts. Figure 12.1 shows the priority audiences for our Libraryland example.

Once you know who your priority audiences are, then you can evaluate what their primary needs and motivators are, and take a close look at what kinds of information they need in order to make a decision to support your request. Figure 12.2 gives you an easy way to walk through each audience group and assess the information that would be most motivating to your audience. It shows the process of analysis using two of the Cityville audience groups.

STEP 3.
Persuasion—Messages and Strategies That Get to Yes

With your purpose and your audience clearly defined, you are ready to move into the action phase of your advocacy planning. This section addresses two parts:

your message and your strategies. The questions you'll answer in forming your messages include

- Why should your audience support your proposal?
- What does your audience need to know in order to take the action you want? (The answer here should align with their values/needs/motivators.)

A message sequence is included in this section that you can adapt for your own use.

Building Effective Messages

Before you get started collecting facts and figures, it is useful to remember how decision making happens. People make decisions first based on how they feel about something (with their heart) and then look for the data to support their emotional choice (with their head). To effectively persuade others, you need *proof* that speaks to both the head and the heart. This head/heart equation is essential to successful messages for any communication effort and is especially critical in building supportive action from your advocacy audiences. Remember, the burden of proof is yours. You simply can't assume people will make the connection between what you have to offer and what they care about. You have to make that link for them and show them how acting in support of your request is acting in support of their own values and interests.

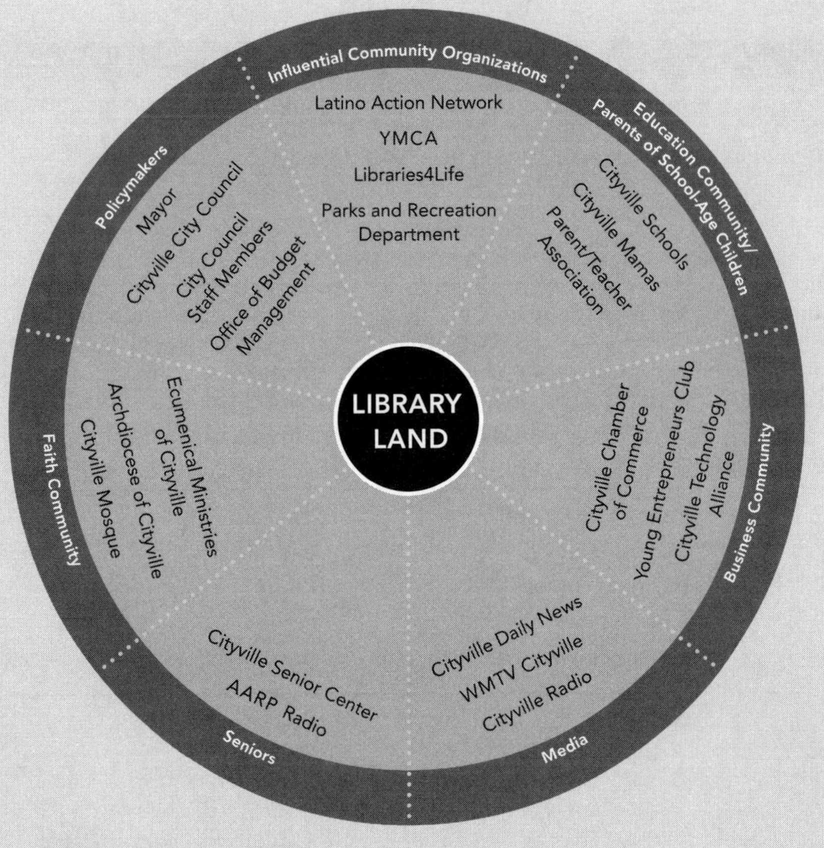

Of course, the best starting point is to determine what the community (broadly) values most. Over the past decade, my organization has worked extensively with libraries using a values-based message platform that connects the library with the things that people already value and are most likely to support; education, economic vitality, health, and stable

FIGURE 12.1 Cityville priority audience wheel

communities are excellent starting points. The section that follows describes an approach to use when building your advocacy messages.

Advocacy messages are most effective when they follow a logical sequence that begins with the ways in which the library affects the things a community already values. It is difficult if not impossible to persuade an individual or a community to adopt a new value. Instead, you must understand how what you are advocating for—in this case, libraries—connects to the things that people already value. Using this sequence and the sample messages in this chapter, you can refine and customize your messages for your specific audiences. Though the exact way a message is delivered will likely change for different audiences, the basics should not.

A common sequence used in effective advocacy is illustrated in figure 12.3 and subsequently described in more detail. Using this sequence to build your messages takes you through a series of steps for building effective arguments that begins with identifying how the library supports key community values and ends with a specific call to action.

1. Value themes: These messages describe how the library affects or benefits the things a community already values. To ensure that this approach is useful to as many types of libraries as possible, the sample messages that we've used focus on the four most broadly held value areas: community vitality and stability, education/lifelong learning, health and well-being, economic health/return on investment. There may be other important values that you see present in your community; if you know what they are, use them. If you don't know, you can conduct a survey or look at other existing community research about priorities to help you refine your approach.

2. Need: These messages define the community need, how the library can meet that need, and what action is required for that to occur.

3. Cost: These messages define the cost or investment required from the audience in order for the library to meet the community need (always in terms as simple as possible; for example, taking the overall budget figure and breaking it down per household, or per individual).

ANALYSIS STEPS	SAMPLE AUDIENCES	
Audience/Segment Who are the people we are trying to reach?	Policymakers (elected officials)	People with school-age children
What do they need to know in order to take action? What are the key motivators?	How the action meets community and constituency expectations; whether action is a wise investment (fiscally responsible)	How the action supports or creates opportunity for success of my child
Who influences this audience? Who do they listen to?	Policymaker's staff Constituents Business leaders Campaign donors Community leaders	Other parents Teachers
Priority Ranking A: Must reach in order to achieve stated goal(s) and/or help us reach other priority audiences. B: Need to reach in order to achieve goals. C: Helpful, but not immediately necessary to achieve goals. Invest less time with them.	A	A

FIGURE 12.2   Cityville audience analysis grid

4. Benefit: These messages describe what the community receives in exchange for the investment made. When you are developing benefit messages, it is important to remember to go back to the value messages in number one. Ultimately, you should be able to illustrate how supporting your proposal results in improvement in areas that your audiences value most:

- community vitality and stability
- education/lifelong learning
- health and well-being
- economic health/return on investment

5. Call to action: These messages ask the audience to take action and support the library. Note: When the decision-making audience is the public, these messages may need to be delivered by library supporters outside the library to ensure that you are respecting the boundaries established for public employees and the use of public resources. However, libraries can and should be actively using the first four elements of the message sequence to educate all their audiences.

One way that you can make the best use of this message framework is to keep the value themes consistent, so that all of your communication efforts reinforce one another. The needs, cost, benefit, and call to action can evolve as your library continues to respond to your community's evolving needs and priorities.

When using and customizing these messages, place yourself in the shoes of members of your audiences. One of the biggest mistakes libraries make is crafting messages that appeal to those on the inside (preaching to the choir). Messages must be tailored to resonate with each specific audience and connect to what motivates them.

Let's look at how our friends at Libraryland have used the sequence in their community. For the sake of this example, we have assumed that the priority value themes in Cityville are education and lifelong learning, followed more distantly by health and community stability.

VALUE THEMES

Libraryland helps create a vital, stable, livable community here in Cityville. (Every story you tell should link back to this theme somehow.)

Libraryland helps residents live healthier lives by providing access to health information, which enables seniors and young families to be better advocates for their own health and well-being and for that of their children and grandchildren. Like many Americans, a significant portion of Cityville residents don't have health insurance, and for them Libraryland is their only health information resource.

Libraryland is a valuable resource to our business community and helps support the vitality and economic health of our community by providing quality online and print resources and adult education that is needed to start and grow businesses and build workforce skills.

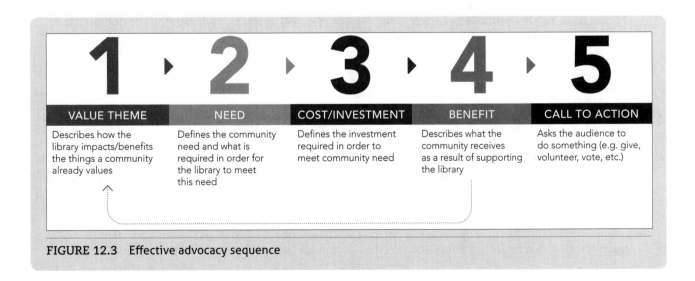

FIGURE 12.3 Effective advocacy sequence

Libraryland delivers an excellent return on community investment.

NEED

Libraryland is committed to meeting the needs of the community. Our recent survey shows that residents want Libraryland to be open seven days a week, need a 25 percent increase in the number of computer terminals to meet demand, want us to add back ESL and early learning programs that were cut last year, and want to see our collection of books, materials, and relevant online databases expand to meet of the diverse needs of our growing community.

To meet this need, Libraryland will require a 7 percent increase from the Cityville general fund, taking the library from 3 percent to 4.5 percent of the city's budget.

COST

To meet the community's needs, the Cityville City Council will need to increase general fund support for the Libraryland budget. (Note: If the city council had predetermined that it would support the increased allocation but would raise taxes to do so, it is important to support that decision and to note the investment from taxpayers to meet this need. The expanded message below addresses this need.)

The Cityville City Council has agreed to expand library funding through a $15 per year, per wage-earner increase in the payroll tax paid by employers.

BENEFIT

The community has asked for increased hours, improved computer access, additional subscription databases for business and research purposes, and more adult learning programs.

Full funding of Libraryland will enable us to meet these growing information and lit-eracy needs and invest in keeping our community strong, stable, and livable.

CALL TO ACTION

Be specific to the audience, but always translate your call to action to a specific form of support. Here are some examples:

- tell a friend
- support the library (volunteer, donate resources or services)
- endorse the library's proposal
- pass the budget
- vote (Note: Before you make a call to action, be sure to check with your legal counsel about what is and is not allowed.)

Using Libraryland as an example, one call to action could be "Write to your city council member and urge his or her support of the mayor's proposed budget increase for the library."

Strategies for Successful Advocacy

Once you have actively defined your messages, it's time to determine how you'll share them and what supporting tools you need. This section discusses the strategies and tools you'll need to implement your advocacy plans.

The questions you'll answer to define strategies include

- Who is the best person or messenger to share this story?
- How can you get the audience to listen to that person(s)?
- What channels of communication are the best for the audience? (not what is the most convenient for you)

Successful strategies and the activities that flow from them can't be created using a cookie-cutter approach, but there are some approaches that are more useful than others and don't cost a small fortune to implement. The most important consideration is to select approaches that are responsive to the needs and preferences of your audiences. The centerpiece of your advocacy strategy is linking the library to existing community values, so you can tap into things people already care about. There are three primary approaches to demonstrating the connection between your library and the values of your community:

1. Direct outreach. Share your message directly with those in your community who have the ability to influence others in favor of your issue or problem and those who are or will be directly affected by your issue.

2. Grassroots outreach/partnership development. Connect with the organizations and businesses that have member, customer, employee, and other types of networks that can join you in advocating for your issue because they share the same or a similar concern.

3. Media and online communication. Use media, websites, e-mails, and other channels to support other forms of outreach and amplify your message.

In addition to these formal approaches, you can use collateral or print materials to get your message out. However, people are most persuaded by *other people*, not posters or fliers. That said, ensure that if you do use print materials, you have a clear plan for distributing them and you are certain that they are in a format that is useful and appropriate to your priority audiences.

It is also worth mentioning that word of mouth and *word of mouse* are among the most powerful and cost-effective approaches. They work by reaching audiences through existing relationships, establishing an endorsement frame, and building momentum. This human capital approach is especially useful because it can be effectively used inside and outside the library by all staff, foundation members, Friends of the Library, etc. Make sure you arm your staff with the information they need to be effective messengers. Talking points and fact sheets that provide easy-to-repeat messages that reflect community values and needs can be great tools for this.

Tools and Tactics That Support Each Approach

The activities and tools described below are grouped together under each of the three approaches so you can see the menu of things you could choose to do in your advocacy efforts. Remember that you are select-ing tools based on what will work with your audience, not just based on what is easy or convenient to do.

1. DIRECT OUTREACH
Direct outreach typically involves individuals or small groups you meet with directly.

In-person meetings. Often the most effective outreach is a direct conversation. One-on-one or small group meetings with a key influencer or decision maker provide the opportunity to make your case, build relationships, and request support in the most powerful way—person-to-person. It is ideal to have an influencer with a direct relationship set up the meeting and participate in it. It is often beneficial to have one to two volunteer advocates (who are peers with the prospective champion) participate in the meeting and make any direct policy and advocacy requests that a library employee cannot or should not make.

Coffees and brown bags. Often used with elected officials or other community leaders, this type of meeting is an informal opportunity to share your point of view.

Meetings/town halls. Elected officials frequently hold meetings or town hall forums when they are in the community. Make sure you attend, recruit members of the community to attend and/or partner with your elected official to create a meeting focused on the value of the library to the community.

Community meetings and public forums. You can use existing community meetings and public forums about a variety of topics (schools, planning, etc.) to demonstrate the value of your public library, or you can create your own to talk specifically about the library. If you are trying to gather information about the needs of your community, these are good places to reach an informed and interested citizen population.

Staff/committee meetings. Elected officials have staff who deal with specific community issues and also serve on committees. In addition to connecting directly with your elected officials, form relationships with their policy staff.

Library and partner events. Utilize library and partner events to demonstrate the value of the library. Opportunities include back-to-school nights, author events, faculty events, etc.

Program outreach. Use existing program outreach, such as the bookmobile, to share your messages about the value of the library.

Speakers bureaus. Create a speakers bureau of trained library messengers that can advocate for the library at a wide range of events.

Let's look at how Libraryland and its partner Libraries4Life used this direct outreach approach as a major focus of the work done by Libraryland to secure funding from Cityville. The first step the library took was to talk with library leadership in the branches who had been involved in the recent community assessment and to confirm the library board's approval of plans to secure increased funding from the city. The staff leadership created a biweekly update that they sent out to keep staff informed of the progress of the funding effort, to demonstrate the key messages, and to provide updates from the library board chair and from the volunteer leaders of Libraries4Life.

Libraries4Life then worked with the library to host coffees with key influencers and meet one-on-one with Cityville City Council members, as well as to attend regular meetings of the city council. They recruited key business, neighborhood, and education leaders to attend and testify at town hall forums about the city budget. In addition, information handouts that explained the library's goal of expanding services and resources to meet community needs were available at all library programs and at joint programs conducted by the library and the chamber.

2. Grassroots Outreach

Building a relationship with another community organization can result in the use of new communication channels that amplify or convey your message to many members of their network and community. Grassroots outreach often involves making connections through a partner or ally in the community such as Boys and Girls Clubs, schools, the YMCA, and community centers. Grassroots outreach can also be conducted directly to your volunteer, donor, and support base.

Action alerts. Best utilized once a stakeholder group is engaged and becomes part of your grassroots network, these short messages are used to motivate action about a time-sensitive issue that requires immediate attention. The call to action usually involves contacting an elected official or media outlet to advocate for the desired action.

Phone campaigns. This campaign technique can be conducted by issuing an action alert asking participants to contact a person or group and/or by convening in a phone bank location, such as an office with enough phone lines to have multiple callers making calls at the same time, and having volunteers call a predetermined list of people.

Partner mailings/postings. You can expand communication channels by acquiring mailing lists and/or including library information in partner publications and by using partners' e-mails and websites.

Hearings. Public hearings are held by many policy-making bodies and are a critical forum to ensure that the right messengers (diverse community members and influencers of the decision makers) are in attendance and deliver testimony that conveys the advocacy message and becomes part of the public record.

Lobby days. A group or coalition of groups with similar interests organizes a lobby day to gather a large number of people at a capitol/city hall/county seat to conduct personal meetings with elected officials about a key issue or upcoming vote.

In our example, Libraries4Life took the lead on the grassroots outreach aspect of the advocacy work for Libraryland by connecting with several local groups including Cityville Mamas (an education advocacy group), the Latinos Action Network (one of the community's largest cultural institutions), as well as the local YMCA and the Young Entrepreneurs Club. (Each of the groups had previously held community forums on behalf of the library where community members shared their ideas and needs with library representatives.) Libraries4Life asked these partners, as well as the Cityville Chamber of Commerce and the Cityville public schools, to host information sessions and share materials with their constituencies via mailings, e-mail, and websites. They agreed to work with Libraries4Life to distribute information about the library's plan to expand resources and address needs to endorse this important community investment. They also formed a joint opinion-leaders task force that met personally with elected officials, and attended budget and other council meetings to advocate on behalf of library funding.

3. Media Outreach

Media outreach includes using formal and informal media channels to extend the reach of your message. You may be familiar with a broad array of media relations tools. The information provided here focuses on the ways in which media can most effectively be used in support of advocacy efforts.

Editorial board visits. Request a meeting with the editorial staff of a publication to share your story and ask for an editorial endorsing your position and urging their readers to take action (vote, call their city council member, etc.).

Editorials. The official opinion of the newspaper, these articles appear in the editorial section of the paper. They are developed by editorial staff, but can be influenced by advocates. Your goal is to get the editorial group to write a positive editorial about your issue.

Op-ed (opposite the editorials). These signed opinion pieces are submitted to an editorial page for consideration. They can be submitted by a library director, board, Friends of the Library, or other library advocates.

Letters to the editor. These may be responses to editorials or key issues in a community that can be submitted for editorial page publication. (Remember, not everything requires a response.)

News announcement. These announcements are the official way to release news to the media. Your news must be factual and timely.

Feature pitches. Pitching (usually with a memo, e-mail or conversation) an idea to reporters, editors, or producers to write a story on an issue, trend, personality, or other relevant story that builds the case for the need, the library's value related to the need, or increases understanding of a key service.

Public service announcements. These announcements inform the public about safety and health information, community services, or public affairs.

Radio and TV programming. This includes appearing on local radio or TV current events programs to talk about your issue.

Paid advertising. While not traditionally something most libraries can afford, supporting groups may use this tool to reinforce the library's message. This tool can include print, radio, television, outdoor, transit, and/or web-based advertisements.

Web. This includes your own website as well as those of media or partners.

E-mail campaign. A letter-writing campaign can be conducted using e-mail.

Blogs. Although community blogs are a more informal tool than your website, they are often widely read by respected opinion leaders.

Intranet (your own and those of partners). Internal websites (not available to the public) are another information outlet for messages about the library.

Libraries4Life again played an active role in working with library leadership to visit editorial boards, write letters to the editor, share information in their own websites and intranets, and ultimately convince the three former mayors of Cityville to write a joint opinion editorial that was published in the local paper advocating for expanded library resources. Other partners used their websites to post information endorsing the library budget increase and e-mailed their constituents asking for their support. The editorial was leveraged by all of the partners by putting links on their own websites to the newspaper's online version. This particular campaign did not employ advertising as a tool because it was not the most effective way to reach the goal.

STEP 4.
Performance—Measuring Your Success

Measurement and evaluation are critical tools for understanding how your advocacy efforts affected your goals. Too often, this step is skipped because it seems difficult, unnecessary, or self-evident (i.e., we got the funding). Whether your efforts succeeded beyond your wildest expectations, failed miserably, or hit somewhere in the middle, measurement and evaluation can help you understand what worked—and what didn't—and how to adapt your strategy appropriately. In ongoing advocacy efforts, measurement can serve as ongoing touch points in a constant process of evaluation and evolution.

The first step in successful measurement and evaluation is setting goals and objectives that are measurable. The second is knowing your starting point—just one more reason to conduct even a simple community survey.

There are two primary ways to measure your accomplishments: process measures and outcome measures. Process measures look at activity (how many people attended open houses, how many fact sheets were distributed, etc.) while outcome measures look at what is different as a result (number of positive votes on the city council, actual policy and budget change, number of advocates and endorsing organizations, etc). Each is a valid measure in its own right, but to create better understanding of what happened and why, you should measure and analyze both.

Sample Process Measures (What did you do?)

- How much "stuff" did you create, including fliers, postcards, bookmarks, brochures, media material, etc.?
- Where and to whom did you distribute your materials?

- Did you conduct outreach? To how many people and where?
- Did you engage the media? If so, which ones and with what frequency?
- Did you engage your staff, board, administration, other leadership of your institution (if you are an academic library), Friends of the Library, or foundations? If so, how?

Sample Outcome Measures (What happened?)

- Did you achieve your end goal?
- How many people saw your materials?
- Did you receive positive media stories?
- Did you earn endorsements from other organizations or individuals? If so, who?
- Who got involved? What did they do?

You can gather this information formally through surveys, interviews, or focus groups, or informally, based on your own anecdotal evidence. Using both approaches will give you the fullest range of information. Having this information available will help you assess what worked, what didn't, and most important what you know about *why*, so that you can make adjustments in your approach as you continue the important advocacy and communication work for your library.

Get Going!

Walk yourself through the steps outlined in this chapter. Ask yourself the questions and build your plan for successful advocacy. Whether you are advocating for funding for an issue that affects your library's service delivery or to improve the perception of the library and build public support for future needs, you have a critical role to play. You must be a library advocate because if those closest to the library aren't championing the library's role in meeting community need, why should anyone else? Furthermore, you and your colleagues have a unique perspective on how the library is used, how it changes people's lives, and how it addresses community needs. You can also convert other community stakeholders to be champions and advocates for the library. It is through many voices and many perspectives that the relevance, impact, and importance of the library are best delivered. Remember, the approaches and tools outlined in this chapter are not strategies to be kept in reserve and used every four years when the levy is up or during budget hearings once a year. They are a set of practices that can imbue your ongoing work, community engagement, program delivery, and library communication with additional power.

What you do every day matters. Libraries ensure knowledge and information are free and accessible for all. They ensure opportunity by providing support for educational success, business development, workforce building, and career development. Libraries empower patients and caregivers to advocate for their health, they connect new immigrants to the American dream, and they are the front line in the fight for literacy. Ultimately, libraries provide inspiration, spark imagination, feed our souls, and nurture our communities. Advocacy engages others in the support of these critical societal needs and amplifies the voice of librarians and library advocates as leaders and champions of civil society.

Note

The author acknowledges Metropolitan Group's clients, including the members of the PLA Smartest Card Task Force and the libraries of Washington State, all of whom were instrumental in the refining of the advocacy approach described here; and Eric Friedenwald-Fishman, Jennifer Gilstrap Hearn, Nicole E. Carter, and Jason Petz, who contributed to the development of this advocacy framework. Major portions of this content may be found in toolkit format with worksheets and supporting documentation in *Libraries Prosper with Passion, Purpose and Persuasion,* written by this author and originally published by the Public Library Association, a division of the American Library Association.

13

BUILDING A COMMUNITY
Empowering People as Messengers

Chip Conley and Eric Friedenwald-Fishman

Marketing is about creating relationships. Yet people don't want to be marketed to—they want to build a relationship. A core question every library should ask itself is, "What kind of relationship am I building with my community?"

Old-school marketing was based upon selling products or services. If you were a marketing executive and your company was launching a new product or service, you would call in your ad agency, look for a sexy or manipulative way to gain some "mindshare" from your target audience, and then spend big bucks to sell your audience on why they should want your product. The relationship between company and customer would be purely transactional—not to dismiss the fact that loyalty sometimes would be created in the process.

New-school marketing is based upon satisfying needs. It recognizes that we live in a world of marketing pollution. Pushing product doesn't work any more, especially in the era of the Internet, when savvy customers can connect with each other and trade stories about your programs and services—and your organization—and can easily find alternative choices. Furthermore, it isn't even clear who your target customer is any more because traditional demographics are no longer so predictable, and traditional barriers such as distance have all but disappeared.

In the past, the organization controlled the relationship, but in today's remote-control world, customers are no longer passive. In fact, community members have never been so powerful. And after years of being manipulatively marketed to, customers have a healthy skepticism about most organizations—and they should.

During the last four decades, Americans have had cause to be skeptical of all of our traditional institutions, from government to religion to media to business. These institutions have not been consistently trustworthy. So today's newly powerful community members, who still desire and search for deeper relationships and meaning, look for institutions they can trust, and they respond to communication that offers a relationship. Increasingly, effective communication relies upon empowering people as messengers.

Imagine an experiment with a pair of identical twins walking down the street in the same direction—one of the twins on one side of the street and the other on the opposite side. One wears a T-shirt with the Dell logo emblazoned on it, while the other wears a T-shirt with an Apple logo on his chest. Over the course of walking a few blocks on a crowded city street, how many familiar reactions (a wink, a nod, a smile) will the Apple twin get as compared to the Dell twin? While both companies are well respected for their technology, Apple has a cult-like following and has created a community of cheerleaders who live and breathe the brand. And no doubt, this community is more likely to nod or smile to one of its brethren.

Building a community of believers is one of the best pieces of marketing advice we can give to any organizational leader. Keeping this advice in mind will undoubtedly serve both your funding and your social impact aspirations. According to consulting giant McKinsey and Company, about two-thirds of all economic activity in the United States is influenced by people's shared opinions about a product, brand, or service.[1] It's logical that the people who are most likely to share an opinion are the true believers who feel themselves to be part of a brand's community. And, of course, word of mouth recommendations are not just more influential—and considered to be more trustworthy—but they're dramatically less expensive than any other form of marketing. More and more, "source credibility" defines whether your potential customers, stakeholders, and voters believe what they hear about your library or whether they take it with a grain of salt.

What if you had to tell your story nine times before your best friend acknowledged what you were saying? For one, you'd probably pick a new best friend. But that's a good way of looking at the inherent flaws in traditional advertising. Conventional wisdom suggests that it takes nine impressions for an audience member to retain information in an ad. One good story from a friend far outweighs the potential of nine expensive ads.

This chapter focuses on empowering people as messengers. In it, we illustrate key points with stories both from libraries and from private companies that are demonstrating cutting-edge application of this approach. At the end of the chapter we suggest three core applications to help you put these ideas into practice. The key point of this chapter is to help you build a community—a credible source—that's committed to your library. That community is larger than just your most loyal library users. Good word of mouth also comes from employees, strategic partners, community leaders, professionals in fields related to library services (education, social services, community development, etc.), and the media. Engage all of these constituencies and you have the makings of what author Douglas Atkin and others now refer to as a cult brand.[2]

Cult Brands

Cult brands are not the only organizations that receive positive word of mouth, but they are the ones that create the greatest bang for the buck. So let's study what makes a cult brand and how it engages its followers by creating a sense of community. What makes a cult brand? There are four common characteristics that you'll find in any cult brand: (1) a differentiated product or service; (2) an empowered employee and customer base that appreciates being part of something outside the mainstream; (3) a renegade or underdog message; and (4) an easy ability to join the community. Dell is a commodity while Apple is differentiated. United Way is seen as commodity while MoveOn.org and Habitat for Humanity are seen as differentiated. Commodities speak to the mainstream and don't create cult brands. Cult brands emerge when an organization launches an unusual product or service that captures the fascination of a certain niche of customers in the marketplace. For example, the reintroduced Volkswagen Beetle and the MINI Cooper created huge fervor from a segment of car buyers, just as the release of each Harry Potter edition had families lined up at bookstores at midnight, with long wait lists for the book and packed special events.

Enthusiastic employees and customers who feel emotionally associated with this kind of differentiated brand are a powerful cornerstone of a cult brand. Cult branders know that they're not just selling a product or service, but they're also connecting with the dreams, passions, and aspirations of their employees and customers. The power of association or the sense of belonging is a deep need in all humans and one that cult brands do a wonderful job of satisfying.

Most cult brands start with a shoestring budget and a David vs. Goliath worldview. The combination of that underdog philosophy with a renegade message or product means that in-the-know customers recognize how important they are to the company's future success. The fastest way to create evangelical customers is to make them feel that their voice is heard—and essential.

A simple example of this comes from the origins of the popular British company, Innocent Drinks. Three young blokes decided they wanted to quit their boring jobs in advertising and management consulting and start a smoothie business. They set up a stand at a small music festival in London and put up a big sign that read: "Do you think we should give up our jobs to make these smoothies?" They put out one trash bin that said, "YES" and one that said "NO" and asked people to discard their empty bottles into the "YES" or "NO" bin. They got very quick and detailed customer feedback, and now, just a few years later, they've built their company into one of the United Kingdom's best-known socially responsible cult brands.[3]

Library programs like Summer Reading have often started with shoestring budgets and, in many communities, have become defining community programs. In Indianapolis and Portland, Oregon—cities with less than eight hundred thousand people—more than fifty thousand kids consistently participate in Summer Reading.

Finally, the last common characteristic of cult brands is that they welcome everyone who's interested into their community. Harley-Davidson appeals to all types and has created the well-known Harley Owners Group (H.O.G.) as a means for Harley owners to connect with each other and share their love of the product. In the same way, One Book or Everybody Reads programs have connected entire communities—spanning every demographic—to a book or author and to ideas relevant to community needs through their library. This is easier to do when you have a lifestyle-driven product that naturally encourages a gathering of community—and libraries by their very nature fit this bill.

How Cult Brands Use Their Websites

The Internet is the perfect medium for furthering the conversation between organizations and their most enthusiastic customers. Check out the website of any marketing-savvy, socially responsible company and we bet you'll find many ways to engage with the community that orbit around that company or brand. One of our favorites is Clif Bar's website (www.clifbar.com), where you can click on "Play" and get information on a variety of sponsored events and the two thousand

Team Clif Bar athletes. The site also has a blog that's populated with the Clif Bar community talking about everything from the state of the world to the state of Clif's newest product launch.

Or visit Chicago Public Library's website (www.chipublib.org). Immediately you are encouraged to engage with the library on your own terms with the bold section headings: Read, Learn, and Discover. The library invites participation in numerous events and programs with a frequently updated broad selection of exciting upcoming programs featured at the top of the home page. Users are also encouraged to comment on the website by clicking on a "tell us what you think" box on the home page.

A Community-Building Success Story

Let's take a closer look at one company that is a role model for creating community. You will see in this example many similarities to the perspective and choices that drive effective marketing for libraries: a focus on education versus promotion; the importance of building trust by delivering results; creating opportunities and empowering others to tell the story; integrating increasingly diverse ways of accessing services; and building relationships with patrons rather than focusing on transactions.

More than forty years ago, Patagonia founder Yvon Chouinard produced his first mail order catalog, a one-page mimeographed sheet of adventure gear with a note to potential customers advising them not to expect fast delivery during climbing season. Patagonia is now an international organization with annual sales that exceed $250 million, but it still feels like a funky, homegrown little company.

Does Patagonia have a differentiated product? In Yvon Chouinard's manifesto, *Let My People Go Surfing: The Education of a Reluctant Businessman,* he writes, "Striving to make the best quality product is the reason we got into business in the first place. We are a product-driven company, and without a tangible product there would obviously be no business . . . because we had a history of making the best climbing tools in the world, tools that your life is dependent on, we couldn't be satisfied making second-best clothing."[4]

Patagonia is not only intent on creating the best product, but it also has a stated goal of causing "no unnecessary harm." In the 1990s, Patagonia's managers embarked on an effort to understand the life cycle impacts of the four major fibers used in its products:

polyester, nylon, cotton, and wool. What they found surprised them as they learned that conventionally grown cotton had as negative an environmental impact as synthetic fibers and wool. The company took more than one-third of its employees, as well as many of its suppliers, on a tour of cotton fields to make it clear why Patagonia had to make the expensive switch to using only organic cotton in the production of its clothing.

Once this decision was made—years before other, much larger companies disclosed their "dirty laundry"—Patagonia wrote in its next catalog, "Everything we do pollutes." The company unveiled its plan to change production methods and hinted at a cost implication for taking this environmentally responsible step. Patagonia's openness about the negative impact of its production created a high level of trust among its employees and managers. It further engaged the 20 percent of its customers (based upon Patagonia's market research) whose buying patterns are heavily influenced by the values of a company they purchase from.

Does Patagonia have an empowered employee and customer base that feels different? Patagonia's employee retention is four times better than the industry averages for retail companies, so clearly it has happy employees.

Does Patagonia have a renegade message? Chouinard's book title certainly has a renegade spirit to it. On its website under "Environmentalism," you can read about how you can make a difference regarding global warming or the Arctic National Wildlife Refuge. In 2004, Patagonia's customers sent fifteen thousand letters to President George Bush asking him to take out the four dams on the Snake River that were key to restoring salmon to that river system.

Patagonia's message has influenced how it uses its catalog and website in its marketing. Over the years, Chouinard writes in his book, "We have come upon a balance we find just about ideal: 55 percent product content and 45 percent devoted to message—essays, stories, and image photos. Whenever we have edged that content toward increased product presentation, we have actually experienced a decrease in sales."[5]

Does Patagonia make it easy for people to join its community? Yes, and in so many ways. For example, it puts a notice in the catalog asking customers and photographers to "capture a Patagoniac" in the midst of adventure using the company's products. The company has been inundated with photos that have become catalog content and helped customers feel like they were a part of the Patagonia culture (certainly more authentic than hiring an expensive model). Customers are also encouraged to participate in adventure events in far-flung places.

Since 1985, Patagonia has pledged 1 percent of its annual sales to organizations that are helping to preserve and restore the natural environment. The company has awarded nearly $20 million in grants to domestic and international grassroots groups that are making a difference in their local communities. More recently, Patagonia helped create "1% for the Planet," an alliance of two hundred businesses that have committed to donating 1 percent of annual revenues to environmental causes. This is just one more way for Patagonia customers to feel like they are part of the unique community that orbits around this company.

As a cult brand, how does Patagonia approach the subject of marketing? The company has three general guidelines that define its promotional efforts:

1. "Our charter is to inspire and educate rather than promote."

2. "We would rather earn credibility than buy it. The best resources for us are the word-of-mouth recommendations from a friend or favorable comments in the press."

3. "We advertise only as a last resort."[6]

These same guidelines are in perfect alignment for the most effective marketing by libraries.

Based upon this promotional strategy, Patagonia estimates it receives press coverage that would be comparable to about $7 million in annual advertising costs. The company has learned through trial and error how to develop successful promotional campaigns. From Patagonia's learning, we've been able to identify three steps the company takes to support its community's ability to spread word of mouth and connect with the company:

Step 1. Learn where your word of mouth comes from. The company's marketing team uses online and e-mail surveys to understand more about its customers' behavior and opinions. What it initially found was that about half of Patagonia customers eventually recommend the brand to others, but that it takes some time before this word of mouth kicks in. It takes a while for customers to realize how durable the products are, and they don't have enough opportunities to engage with the brand (given the low-key advertising and the fact that there are fewer than twenty retail stores in the United States). This research also found that the most evangelical customers were those who knew the most about the company's core values. The result of this research was that Patagonia decided to step up its messaging on its website and in its catalog and to provide as many means as possible for customers to interact with the brand.

Step 2. Develop cross-channel customer visibility and interaction. Patagonia has various distribution channels: its own stores, its website, its catalog, and its wholesale business in other stores. Prior to doing the research in Step 1, these four distribution channels operated relatively independently of each other, so there weren't many opportunities to integrate customer data across channels. Once Patagonia studied this data, it found catalog customers who lived or worked within blocks of one of its retail stores. It reached out and invited these customers to visit the store to build a deeper connection with the company. This also meant Patagonia had to redefine the return on investment since these four channels were no longer unconnected silos and now supported the whole marketing mission.

Step 3. Refocus communications from the transaction to the relationship. In the era of the Internet, there's less need for the catalog to be the primary method of spreading the message. This also means a company can look at ways to reduce the size of its catalog, which is a socially responsible thing to do. As mentioned before, the Patagonia website has an authentic voice and is focused on creating a relationship. The home page has as many links to information on the company's environmental initiatives as it has links to its store and product pages. Its press section doesn't harp on sales records or product announcements, but is more focused on what Patagonia is doing for the community. At the core of this marketing strategy is the belief that its website is a conversation between company and customer. Patagonia is so focused on making sure its website is an effective tool for building community that it occasionally pulls customers out of its retail stores, sits them down in front of a computer, and gives them a gift certificate. Then these customers shop on the website while Patagonia staff watches and records their comments as valuable information. This very personal, in-depth approach to getting inside its customers' heads has helped Patagonia create one of the most successful, socially responsible retail websites.

Don't despair if your library hasn't yet built a business model that's as customer-empowering as Patagonia's. It's a beacon in the socially responsible community, but there's no reason you can't start using some of its best practices to help create a powerful community that supports what you do. Libraries have many opportunities to learn from their users, to integrate and communicate value across on-site, online and outside-the-building program experiences, and to build authentic relationships where users experience their library as a trusted partner and an organization in which they are owners, as opposed to a transaction point for books, materials, and information.

Core Applications

To successfully build a community, you need to engage three different groups:

1. Empower your employees as messengers.

2. Empower your customers and community as messengers.

3. Empower your strategic partners as messengers.

Empower Your Employees as Messengers

From Google to Microsoft, many tech companies have created a new title and position in their ranks: the customer evangelist. The role of these evangelists is to engage in an ongoing dialogue with their companies' most important customers about how the companies can serve them better and how they, as customers, can spread the word. Recognizing that it costs five times more to acquire a customer than it does to keep a customer, this approach to marketing just makes good financial sense. Today, companies aren't just focused on branding; they're focused on bonding with their customers as well.

Ben McConnell, coauthor of *Creating Customer Evangelists*, says, "If word of mouth is the skeleton, then customer evangelism is the soul."[7] He and his wife and coauthor, Jackie Huba, cite an example of O'Reilly Publishing, a technical book publisher that created the O'Reilly Evangelist Program with a marketing employee named Simone Paddock taking the lead in identifying customers who were already evangelists (by gathering names from other employees or doing a Google search to see what customers were saying about O'Reilly's books). Simone invited these loyal customers to help design this program, with special focus on how bloggers could spread the news. She asked them what they needed and learned that these evangelist bloggers wanted galley copies of the books, early copies, and they wanted to go to the O'Reilly conferences so they could report on them. Simone set all up all of this and created a newsletter exclusively for this group of customer evangelists.

Do you have to go to the expense of hiring a customer evangelist for your library? Not necessarily. You just need to make sure your line-level employees are empowered to be advocates for your services. Bank of America learned that online banking customers are 11 percent more satisfied than bank customers, 20 percent more likely to purchase additional products and services, and 34 percent more likely to recommend their bank's website. So Bank of America did everything it could to make sure their employees used the bank's online services for their own personal accounts, and by 2004, 90 percent of Bank of America employees used the Internet banking channel. The bank cites this as a major reason that 70 percent of Bank of America's new customers sign up for online banking, a higher percentage than the national average. By using the channel themselves, the tellers and call center agents are the messengers.[8] Now bring this example inside your library: Have you made sure all of your staff have reserved books and made an information query online?

What steps can you take to help your employees become evangelizing messengers? First and foremost, make sure your employees are not just excited about your service—make sure they're happy in their jobs. If you don't do regular work climate surveys of your employees, you will have no benchmark to understand whether their job satisfaction (and enthusiasm about your services and mission) is growing or declining over time.

Next, make sure you provide great internal communication about what's going on in the library. Are employees in the loop on new programs and services being introduced? Are they made aware of articles written about the library? (This is often how your community learns about news at the library.) Is there a means for them to give real-time feedback about what they're hearing from patrons about your programs and services? Look for ways that you can regularly educate and excite your employees about your library and how you are serving the community; you can't just leave this up to your public information staff or director's office.

Create a dialogue with your employees about the importance of customer word of mouth. Ask them about experiences they've had as customers that led to positive or negative word of mouth and delve deeper into their perception of your library users' current satisfaction with your service and programs. In fact, consider reviewing your customer satisfaction data with line-level employees and get their opinions on what you're hearing from customers. It's amazing how few organizations regularly present these data to the employees who have the most influence on improving these scores.

Talk with employees about how they can identify potential evangelizing library users and how they can pass these names on to their managers or the public information office so the library can strike up a deeper relationship with these potential community champions. Create a contest and give a prize to the line-level employee who identifies the most champions in the month. Employee word of mouth about your library to friends and family is important, but even more important is the way they build a relationship with your customers, which will help determine whether library users become part of your cheerleading squad.

Empower Your Customers as Messengers

Soon after nineteen-year-old Mo Siegel started Celestial Seasonings, the herbal tea company, in 1969, he realized that as a small business he needed to encourage his customers to tell their friends about the teas, because the company didn't have the budget to do any significant advertising. Mo enclosed a note in each box of tea that asked people to serve this tea to their friends and to spread the word. This homespun approach to empowering word of mouth paid off big-time, as the early buzz on Celestial Seasonings was that it was an alternative to the old-time tea companies like Lipton.

More recently, the Maryland Library Association launched the first statewide library card in the nation. The M-Power card featured images from across the state and invited library users to see the new card as a key to empowering their lives and communities. Libraries across the state invited users to share their stories and utilized the excitement created by the bold and beautiful new library cards to create word of mouth.

But beware of the risks associated with empowering your stakeholders. First, if you seek to choreograph your champions, they may feel manipulated. It's one thing for an organization to toot its own horn, but when customers are treated like a ventriloquist's dummy, you risk losing trust.

Second, if you want to empower your customers, you'd better feel pretty confident about your program and service quality—because true empowerment (as in an open source blog on your website that allows customers to comment on the library or library program) means that you'll hear the good, the bad, and the ugly.

Empower Your Strategic Partners as Messengers

Many libraries have strategic partners—whether affiliated education providers (school districts, literacy programs, etc.), nonprofits that serve the same community, sponsors of programs, or suppliers—that can help get your message out.

When Multnomah County Library in Oregon wanted to collect overdue books and seriously delinquent library fines and had a low response rate to mailings and phone calls, the library partnered with Starbucks to offer free coffee drinks to everyone who paid their fines in full within a set period of time. The response was overwhelming, with many of the largest overdue fines in the system being paid off. Many libraries have received support from schools in distributing information and signing up students for Summer Reading. Libraries have also established partnerships with the business community to educate voters about operating levies and bond measures and have partnered with community service organizations to engage new immigrant and non-English-speaking communities.

You may have existing strategic partners or you may not. The key features of a great strategic marketing partnership are a common demographic or psychographic community shared by the two organizations, an offer that provides a synergistic benefit to community members, and parallel goals that create mutual gains for the two organizations.

Empower People as Messengers

Whether it's you, your colleagues, staff, policymakers, voters, library patrons, or the media, every person who comes into contact with your library is a potential storyteller for your brand. It's one thing to hear people talk about a great program or service—it's an eye- and mind-opener to hear someone share about a love affair they're having with an organization and/or how they feel about belonging to a real community as a champion of their library. This is the Holy Grail for any organization. And libraries have an advantage in creating this level of relationship based upon their ability to meet diverse community and individual needs, their promise of providing access to opportunity, and their core value and values proposition—everyone's gateway to the world of ideas where knowledge and information are free and accessible to all. Harness the most powerful marketing medium in support of your library's mission by empowering people as messengers.

Notes

This chapter is adapted from text excerpted from *Marketing That Matters: 10 Practices to Profit Your Business and Change the World,* by Chip Conley and Eric Friedenwald-Fishman (San Francisco Berrett-Koehler, 2006).

1. Kevin A. Clark, *Brandscendence: Three Essential Elements of Enduring Brands* (Chicago: Dearborn Trade, 2004).
2. Douglas Atkin, *The Culting of Brands* (New York: Portfolio, 2004).
3. Laura Cummings, "Business Reporter," BBC News Online, July 9, 2003.
4. Yvon Chouinard, *Let My People Go Surfing: The Education of a Reluctant Businessman* (New York: Penguin, 2005).
5. Ibid.
6. Ibid.
7. Ben McConnell and Jackie Huba, *Creating Customer Evangelists: How Loyal Customers Become a Volunteer Sales Force* (Chicago: Dearborn Trade, 2003).
8. Phillip Britt, "Online Banking Clicks with Customers," *CRM Magazine,* November 18, 2004.

14

FRIENDS GROUPS CAN HELP LIBRARIES PROMOTE THEIR SERVICES

Sally Gardner Reed

Every day across the country, Friends of the Library groups are working to help improve their libraries. Mostly, Friends are known for raising thousands of dollars each year through used books sales, ticketed programs and events, and membership dues—money that they make available to the library to supplement its operating budget. Friends may be less appreciated for their ability to promote the library—its programs, services, and value to the community.

While library promotion may not be the first thing you think of when you think of Friends, perhaps it should be. As we know, excellent library promotion can and often does lead to very effective advocacy efforts such as rallying a community to vote in favor of library funding. (See figures 14.1 and 14.2.)

Friends can truly amplify the library's message in the community by ensuring that everyone knows what the library does and, importantly, why what the library does matters to everyone in the community.

If you haven't discussed library promotion with your Friends group, now is the time to talk to them about marketing and public awareness initiatives and even involve them in the development of your campaign. Use your Friends group as a focus group; involve your Friends in developing your message. As members of the "laity," they will undoubtedly have a great perspective on what will resonate with the public at large. What sounds important and powerful to librarians may not sound so to people who have lives beyond the library.

In addition, there may be members of your Friends group who have expertise in areas that can help you craft and then deliver your message. Marketing and promotion techniques from members of the business world are usually transferable. Most important, by involving your key support group in the development of your message, you will go a long way in ensuring they take the lead in delivering it.

In the public library world, Friends are constantly working with their libraries on promotional activities. The Public Library Association's "Smartest Card" and "Every Child Ready to Read @ your library" campaigns have been funded and promoted by Friends groups all across the country. Other campaigns abound. The Friends of the Milwaukee (Wisconsin) Public Library, for example, launched a campaign called, "What a Difference My Library Makes" with brochures, postcards, posters, and fliers featuring photos of library patrons using the library. (See figures 14.3 and 14.4.)

Friends groups can be extremely creative. The Citizens for Maryland's Libraries sponsored a booth at the Baltimore Book Festival promoting the theme, "Quench your thirst for knowledge at the library" complete with "Quench Your Thirst" bottled water giveaways. And much like Chicago's Cows on Parade sculpture project, the Friends of Berks County (Pennsylvania) Libraries used library cats to bring attention and additional dollars to their library. (See figure 14.5.)

Friends across the United States

Here are a variety of examples that can inspire you to develop partnerships of all types with your Friends group.

Carmel, Indiana

The Friends Library Store at the Carmel Clay Public Library commissioned one hundred signed and numbered special edition prints of a mural entitled Nature's Gateway, which was recently installed in the children's story-time room at the library. The full-color reproductions, professionally photographed, have been matted and framed and are ready for hanging. As a bonus, each mural purchase comes with a free one-year coupon for a family-level Friends membership.

Rockville, Maryland

"Born to Read" is a major project of the Friends of the Library in Montgomery County. The program reaches out to parents and babies, especially at-risk families, and teaches them to love books. Sessions held in the library show parents, caregivers, and babies how much fun reading and books can be. One source of funding for the program is donations, and the Friends help to encourage gifts by placing a bookplate in a children's

FIGURE 14.1 Fliers developed by Citizens for Better Libraries, Fargo, N.D., in support of a library funding ballot measure.

FIGURE 14.2 Excellent library promotion can and often does lead to very effective advocacy efforts.

book for a donation. It's a great way to recognize a birthday, anniversary, or other special occasion, and grandparents can use this as a wonderful way to welcome a special child.

Random Lake, Wisconsin

Friends of the Lakeview Community Library promised to raise funds toward the renovation of the town auditorium so it could be turned into a library. They held "endless fund-raisers," which included bake sales, pizza sales, candy sales, rummage sales, quilt raffles, pancake breakfasts, a holiday homes tour, a "Kids R Kute" contest, along with a Cabin Fever Reliever (a local talent show), tulip bulb sales, Christmas holly sales, Valentine's Day cheesecake sales, used book sales, and a campaign for direct contributions. They even offered a series of ballroom dance lessons to prepare for the upcoming Library Ball!

Hutchinson, Kansas

In "Books a la Carte," the Friends of the Hutchinson Library were able to increase the visibility of their organization in the library and in the community, and KOCH Industries was interested in supporting education and literacy. The result was a $2,500 grant to fund the purchase of a merchandise cart that can be used at Friends' sales locations, in the library between sales,

and at local community events to publicize the library and to sell memberships, books, and library items.

Rockford, Michigan

"Baseball Is Back!" for Friends of the Krause Memorial Library, as they began another season of Fantasy Baseball. Participants of all ages filled their team's rosters with the major league players they felt would perform well during the coming season. Six-team divisions were formed. The action began on opening day and continued until the All-Star Break, with the statistics reported for the "real" game used to determine team points and division standings, which are posted every Friday at the library. Grand Rapids native and author William Brashler (*The Bingo Long Traveling All-Stars and Motor Kings*) appeared at the library to discuss his baseball-themed books to launch the effort.

South Windsor, Connecticut

"The Daily Grind: The Real Scoop on Coffee" was presented by the South Windsor Friends. Two speakers from a local coffee shop shared the history and lore of coffee. Sample sips were provided, along with tasty treats provided by the Friends, who invited all attendees to bring a favorite coffee-flavored treat or coffee-go-along to add to the tasting table. Door prizes donated by eleven local businesses added to the fun.

FIGURE 14.3   One of the many posters, postcards, brochures, and fliers featuring library users from "What a Difference My Library Makes!"—a publicity campaign launched by the Friends of the Milwaukee Public Library.

FIGURE 14.4   "What a Difference My Library Makes!" poster. In the public library world, Friends often work with their libraries on promotional activities.

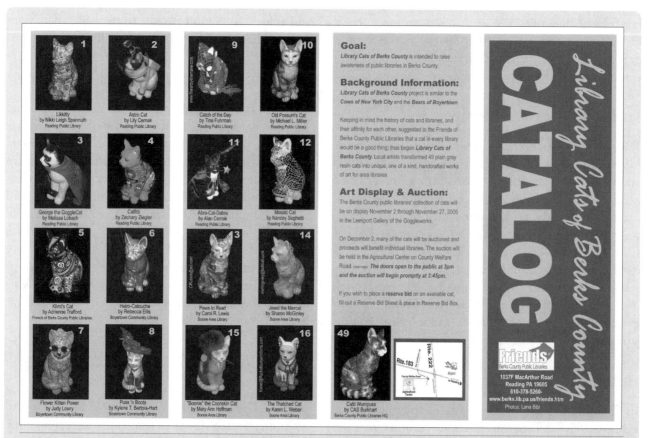

FIGURE 14.5 Friends groups can be very creative. "The Cats of Berks County," an art display and auction, helped raise awareness of public libraries. It was organized by the Friends of Berks County Public Libraries.

Of course the money Friends groups raise is great, but in the long run they can do even more by helping to promote the library, increasing its visibility and ultimately creating a fertile field for convincing members of the community and those who fund libraries about the critical need to fully support the library in good times and, especially, in bad.

For more information on Friends' activities, visit www.folusa.org.

CONTRIBUTORS

Stephen Abram, MLS, is vice president, innovation, for SirsiDynix. He is the chief strategist for the SirsiDynix Institute (www.sirsidynixinstitute.com), an SLA Fellow, president 2008 of SLA, and the past president of the Ontario Library Association and the Canadian Library Association. He is the author of *Out Front with Stephen Abram* and blogs at http://stephenslighthouse .sirsidynix.com. Stephen would love to hear from you at stephen.abram@sirsidynix.com.

Maria Elena Campisteguy is an executive vice president/principal of Metropolitan Group and leads its multicultural communication practice. She brings to her work three decades of experience with communities of color, immigrant populations, and youth as an advocate, marketer, program developer, coach, and consultant. Internationally, she has worked throughout Latin America, Africa, and Japan. More recently she has worked with some of the nation's leading Latino advocacy, education, and media organizations.

Chip Conley is founder and CEO of Joie de Vivre Hospitality, Northern California's largest hotelier. Chip has won numerous awards, including Guerrilla Marketer of the Year from the American Travel Marketing Executives, Northern California Entrepreneur of the Year, National Humanitarian Hospitality Company of the Year, and the Experience Stager of the Year. He is the author of *The Rebel Rules: Daring to Be Yourself in Business, Business Rules of Thumb* (with Seth Godin), and *Peak.*

Laura K. Lee Dellinger is an award-winning and nationally recognized leader in strategic communication. She leads Metropolitan Group's strategic communication practice and has worked with hundreds of members of the library community including state libraries, public libraries, academic and research libraries, and school libraries. She is the principal author of *Libraries Prosper with Passion, Purpose and Persuasion,* a PLA advocacy toolkit.

Eric Friedenwald-Fishman is the creative director and president of Metropolitan Group. He is widely recognized as one of the nation's most effective experts in developing and implementing strategic communication and resource development campaigns that engage diverse stakeholders and get results. He specializes in creating major public will building campaigns that build lasting social change. Eric has twenty years of experience working with public, academic and special collections libraries and archives. He has worked with library associations, foundations, and friends groups throughout the United States and has been a frequent speaker at library conferences.

Megan Humphrey is the manager of the Campaign for America's Libraries, ALA's public awareness campaign that promotes the value of libraries and librarians. Megan has worked for the campaign for eight years, developing tools for libraries around such ALA initiatives as National Library Week and Library Card Sign-up Month, working on partnership programs, programming for conferences, and more. She has a Bachelor of Arts in speech communication from the University of Illinois at Urbana-Champaign.

Chris Kertesz has been writing and editing for more than four decades, as a newspaper copy editor (*Detroit Free Press*), a newsletter editor for the state public health departments of Michigan and Florida, and, for the past twenty years, as a writer for a range of nonprofit agencies.

Dale Lipschultz is the literacy officer in the Office for Literacy and Outreach Services of the American Library Association. Dale focuses on building ALA's capacity in adult literacy by working with the Association's divisions and offices in Chicago and Washington, D.C., supporting the literacy efforts of public libraries in urban centers and rural communities, and collaborating with national partners, government agencies, private funders, and corporate sponsors.

Sally Gardner Reed is the executive director of ALA's Association of Library Trustees, Advocates, Friends, and Foundations.

Michael Steinmacher holds a Bachelor of Arts degree and Masters of Liberal Studies from Bellarmine University, and a Masters of Science in Library and Information Science from the University of Kentucky. He is the manager of branch services for Louisville Free Public Library.

Jené O'Keefe Trigg, managing director at Pro-Media Communications in New York City, has nearly fifteen years of experience in strategic communications management, event production, media relations, and celebrity coordination. She has a degree in Public Relations from the University of Washington.

Steve Zalusky is manager of communications with the American Library Association Public Information Office. Prior to that, he spent twenty years in the newspaper business, as a writer with several publications in suburban Chicago, including Pioneer Press and the *Daily Herald*.

INDEX

You may also be interested in

Small Business and the Public Library: Whether patrons need resources to start their own business, search for a new job, or locate demographic statistics to help them market their existing product, this resource will help you answer questions and meet their needs.

Inside, Outside, and Online: Based on a scan of the community and technology environments within which libraries operate, related literature, and the practical experiences of hundreds of library staff actively building communities through their work, this book provides much-needed insights into the essential elements of community building.

Marketing Today's Academic Library: Written in a concise and engaging manner that speaks to popular anxiety points about new marketing techniques, this book is filled with tips and strategies that academic librarians can use to communicate with students, surpassing students' expectations of their library experience.

Creating Your Library Brand: This book covers everything from working with outside experts to evaluating and maintaining your library's brand, illustrated by case studies from other libraries. For those who have made a start, the chapters stand on their own—librarians can pick up wherever they left off. End-of-chapter exercises enhance the feedback process. Tips, suggestions for success, and answers to frequently asked questions ensure your team collaborates on a library brand that will bring more patrons through the door!

Check out these and other great titles at www.alastore.ala.org!

WITHDRAWN